*Interpersonal Attraction*

# Interpersonal Attraction

ELLEN BERSCHEID
*University of Minnesota*
and
ELAINE HATFIELD WALSTER
*University of Wisconsin*

ADDISON-WESLEY PUBLISHING COMPANY
*Reading, Massachusetts*
*Menlo Park, California · London · Don Mills, Ontario*

TOPICS IN SOCIAL PSYCHOLOGY
Charles A. Kiesler, Yale University, Series Editor

*To Bill and Dewey*

# *Foreword*

It is becoming increasingly difficult for anyone to be a generalist in social psychology. Not only is the number of articles published zooming, but new researchable areas of interest are multiplying as well. A researcher finds more fascinating topics these days than he used to, but he also finds himself behind in his reading of all but one or two of them. As a result, the quality of the broad introductory book in social psychology has suffered. No one can any longer be an expert in all of social psychology.

As an alternative, we offer the present series, *Topics in Social Psychology,* directed toward the student with no prior background in social psychology. Taken as a whole, the series adequately covers the field of social psychology, but it has the advantage that each short book was written by an expert in the area. The instructor can select some subset of the books to make up his course, the particular subset depending upon his biases and inclinations. In addition, the individual volumes can be useful in several ways: as supplementary reading in, perhaps, a sociology course; to introduce more advanced courses (for example, a graduate seminar in attitude change); or just for peeking at recent developments in social psychology.

The present volume centers on interpersonal attraction, running the gamut from attraction and rejection in a group to romantic love. The two personable authors have published numerous articles on these issues and are well-known for their insightful research. In this volume, they consider the general problem of evaluating others—when one person is attracted to another—including such variables as similarity and propinquity of the other and various rewards provided by the other. I think you will find it an exciting book.

Charles A. Kiesler

# Acknowledgments

The authors would like to express thanks to the following publishers for giving them permission to use quotations or figures from their publications: Academic Press, Inc.; American Psychological Association, Inc.; American Sociological Association; Appleton-Century-Crofts, Inc.; Atherton Press, Inc.; Farrar & Rinehart, Inc.; Harcourt, Brace & World, Inc.; Harper & Row, Publishers, Inc.; J. B. Lippincott Company; Scientific American, Inc.; The Society for the Psychological Study of Social Issues; Stanford University Press; John Wiley & Sons, Inc.; and Yale University Press.

# Contents

# CHAPTER ONE

# Introduction

The words "like" and "love," "dislike" and "hate" are among the most frequently used in the English language. Everyone knows what is meant by these terms. Therefore, when we state that we feel "attracted" to a certain person, it is unlikely that we will be asked to define our use of the verb "attracted." It is far more probable that we will be asked *why* it is that a particular person has evoked our positive regard. Probably we will reply by making reference to some of the person's "good qualities" such as his honesty, his sense of humor, or even the cowlick on the back of his head. While explanations referring to qualities which seem to "compel" admiration are frequently given, we shall see that the phenomenon of interpersonal attraction is much more complicated than such explanations would imply. If it were not, this book would consist largely of a listing of all the favorable adjectives in the dictionary. We shall see that although the qualities and behavior of another play a large role in determining whether we will find him attractive, researchers have found that the eye of the beholder is as important as that which is beheld. One must refer to the qualities of the *attracted* as well as to the qualities of the *attracter* to achieve predictive accuracy in interpersonal attraction.

All of the research we will report in this book was conducted in an attempt to answer the general question of *why* people like the people they like. In their search for the determinants of interpersonal attraction, researchers have measured attraction in a great number of different ways. A

Preparation of this chapter was facilitated in part by National Science Foundation Grants 1577 to Berscheid and 1897 to Walster and by the Dean of Students Office, University of Minnesota.

hasty reading of the research might leave the impression that the way one researcher measures "interpersonal attraction" bears little relationship to the way in which another researcher has assessed "interpersonal attraction." Things are not really so chaotic as one might think, however. Almost all experimenters who are interested in interpersonal attraction investigate variables which may affect an individual's positive or negative *attitude* toward another person. These attitudes are sometimes measured by noting where an individual places an X on a scale in response to the question, "How much do you *like* this person?" Sometimes positive or negative attitudes toward another are assessed by noting an individual's tendency to associate with another person, to do favors for another, to glance at another, and so on. The relationship of all these measures to the central construct of "attraction" becomes clearer if we consider for a moment just what psychologists mean when they use the term "attitude."

## ATTITUDE:  A HYPOTHETICAL CONSTRUCT

Although we all have a fairly good idea of what an attitude is, and the word is a working member of almost everyone's vocabulary, many researchers have felt constrained to offer a formal psychological definition of this term. Almost all these definitions have in common the notion that an attitude simply represents a person's readiness to respond toward a particular object, or class of objects, in a favorable or unfavorable manner. For example, Katz and Stotland,* whose definition is perhaps the most concise and contains the essential elements of other definitions, define an attitude as "an individual's tendency or predisposition to evaluate an object or the symbol of that object in a certain way" (1959, p. 428).

The phrase "predisposition to act" appears over and over again with reference to the term attitude. What do we mean by "predisposition to act"? It is interesting to note that the phrase refers, ultimately, to the kinds of predictions that we are going to make about an individual's behavior. For example, when we say that a person has a positive attitude toward the President, generally what we mean is that we have some information which would lead us to predict that in appropriate situations the person will respond in a manner which would support the President. We might predict that the person would boycott the rival party's fund-raising dinners, that he would encourage citizens to vote for the President, and that he is unlikely to think that cartoons which mock the President's programs are as funny as do the President's opponents.

Essentially, then, when we say that we know what a person's attitude

---

*For a complete list of authors quoted, see the *References* at the end of the book.

is, we mean that we have some bits of evidence from the person's past behavior which make us confident that we can predict his future behavior in certain situations. The phrase "predisposition to act," however, implies more than using past behavior to predict future behavior. It is implicit in the phrase that these predispositions are carried around with us; that there is something inside us, perhaps a particular pattern of neural connections, which constitutes our attitude toward the President. These predispositions are thought to exist even when we are not thinking about the President—when we are sleeping, for example, or when we are not in a situation which would call for any action toward his programs. It is for this reason that the concept of attitude as generally defined by most psychologists falls under the category of *hypothetical construct*. A hypothetical construct is a process or entity which is presumed actually to exist, even though it is not directly observable or measurable. One's "attraction" to another is assumed to be a more or less stable characteristic which can be detected from various behaviors in which he engages.

Why have psychologists treated "attitude" as a hypothetical construct? Is it really necessary to refer to some underlying cognitive organization to predict how an individual will behave in a given situation? Why is it not enough to say that because an individual behaved in a favorable way toward a person in the past we predict that he will do the same in the future? Katz and Stotland (1959) have argued that "the term attitude has endured because the practical need for taking account of behavior calls for some stability and for some identifiable affective-cognitive elements which can be related to social behavior in social situations. Thus, the concept of attitude is introduced to allow for the fact that cognitive and affective organization can achieve stability and some degree of constancy." Others might convincingly argue that to treat attitudes as actual entities yields no predictive profit and, in fact, promotes confusion concerning the basis on which we are making behavioral predictions. They argue that since an attitude cannot be directly observed or measured, an attitude itself cannot be used in the prediction of behavior. We can predict future behavior only from observable events.

### *Attraction: A Unidimensional or a Multidimensional Variable?*

Many researchers have assumed that attraction is a unidimensional variable. They assume that attraction and repulsion are mirror images of one another and that the more we dislike someone, the less we like him. In such a conception of "attraction," one's attraction toward another can vary from extreme attraction to extreme repulsion.

A few individuals have considered the possibility that negative and positive feelings toward another might be relatively independent: that one might feel both extreme attraction and extreme repulsion toward the same individual. Though this alternative seems to be a reasonable one, the authors whose work is reported in this book have generally not taken this approach.

## MEASURING ATTITUDES

A multitude of behavioral measures have been used as an index of the attraction, or the positiveness of the attitude, one person has toward another.

The most common technique for assessing an individual's attitude has been to ask him to fill out a self-report questionnaire. For example, Bogardus (1925) developed a scale to measure "social distance," or the closeness of the relationship to which the respondent was willing to admit members of designated social groups. His scale contained seven items, which Bogardus believed denoted seven degrees of permitted closeness. These were:

1.  To close kinship by marriage

2.  To my club as personal chums

3.  To my street as neighbors

4.  To employment in my occupation in my country

5.  To citizenship in my country

6.  As visitors only to my country

7.  Would exclude from my country

Bogardus assumed that in this scale the items were ordered as steps along a continuum—that anyone who agreed with item 5 would almost surely be willing to tolerate others to the extent indicated by items 6 and 7. Presumably from a knowledge of a subject's total score, one could guess how he responded to each item. A scale possessing this property is often labeled a Guttman scale (1944).

Using this scale, Bogardus asked both young businessmen and public school teachers to indicate "In how many groupings in our country may the members of any race, as a class, be admitted?" It is interesting to note how few opportunities for social contact many groups were perceived as possessing in 1925. From Fig. 1.1 it is evident, for example, that in 1925 there was general agreement that an Englishman or a Canadian was much more "socially acceptable" than a Turk or a Negro.*

---

*Bogardus, E. S. "Measuring social distance," *J. Appl. Sociol.*, 1925, **9**, 299-308.

| Races | 1 To close kinship | 2 To club as "chums" | 3 To street as neighbors | 4 To employment in my occupation | 5 To citizenship | 6 As visitors only | Social contact quality indices |
|---|---|---|---|---|---|---|---|
| Armenians | | 3.51 | | | 1.77 | | 6.16 |
| Bulgarians | | 3.97 | | | 1.49 | | 4.62 |
| Canadians | .30 | | 4.55 | | | | 22.51 |
| Chinese | | | 4.28 | | 1.38 | | 4.12 |
| Czecho-Slovak | | 3.46 | | | 1.84 | | 6.20 |
| Danes | 1.48 | | | 3.44 | | | 14.82 |
| English | .27 | | 4.60 | | | | 22.35 |
| French | 1.04 | | | 4.08 | | | 18.67 |
| Germans | 1.89 | | | 3.49 | | | 14.95 |
| Negroes | | | 4.10 | | 1.37 | | 3.84 |
| Japanese | | | 4.30 | | 1 | 1.41 | 4.08 |
| Turks | | | 4.80 | | | 1.18 | 2.91 |

Fig. 1.1. Social contact indices (samples) for selected races, based on reactions of 110 raters. Figures over light lines indicate the social distances before contacts are permitted to the given races. Figures within black bars denote range of the social contacts that are permitted each race.

*Thurstone* (1928) proposed a method of attitude-scale construction which is used by many researchers. It is possible to construct an attitude scale by composing a number of attitude statements, which express a wide range of possible attitudes toward a person or object. For example:

1.   Joe would be intensely disliked by almost any person who came into contact with him.

2.   Joe is a fairly unlikable person.

3.   Joe is a very likable person.

4.   Joe is the kind of person who can get along extremely well with anyone.

A subject is then asked which statement (or statements) best represent his opinion of Joe. The more positive a statement the individual endorses, the more favorable an opinion of Joe he is assumed to have.

Thurstone utilized a technique similar to that described above. His scaling procedure, however, gave his attitude scale some important advantages. He selected his attitude items so that the separation between successive statements of opinion would be uniform. In the haphazardly designed scale we presented above, there is almost surely not a constant increment in favorability from statements 1 to 2 to 3 to 4. Statements 1 and 2 both present fairly similar attitudes toward Joe, while the difference in the attitudes represented by statements 2 and 3 is obviously fairly large.

Thurstone attempted to construct a scale with an evenly graduated series of attitudes in the following way.

First he decided what attitude he wished to measure (for example, "liking for Joe"). Then he wrote or collected 100 opinion statements that seemed intuitively to be related to the specific attitude variable. He wanted to ensure that the statements presented to subjects for endorsement or rejection would cover a wide range of favorableness or unfavorableness, so he purposely included several statements that seemed so extreme that no individual would be likely to endorse them. These 100 opinion statements were printed on small cards. Judges were asked to sort these cards into 11 evenly spaced piles, ranging from (1) opinions most strongly favorable (toward Joe), to (11) those most strongly negative.

Thurstone then excluded from his scale statements whose favorability was found to be ambiguous. If one judge felt that the statement "Joe is the kind of person who can get along extremely well with anyone" was a compliment to Joe, while another judge assumed that the statement must be a criticism of Joe's shallowness and lack of character, this ambiguous item would not be a useful item on an attitude scale, and therefore, it was discarded.

From the remaining statements, Thurstone selected approximately 20 statements which seemed to be evenly graduated along the dimension of favorableness. These statements constituted the attitude scale. Once this scale was in existence, it could be used to measure the attitudes of various individuals toward Joe. Subjects could simply be asked whether they agreed or disagreed with each of the 20 statements. The subject's score was then determined from examination of the degree of favorableness of the statements he had endorsed.

Often, on attitude scales, the individual whose attitude is being assessed is asked to indicate not merely whether he agrees or disagrees with a particular statement, but also *to what extent* he agrees with the opinion statement concerning a person or a group. For example, several studies which have attempted to assess Negro-white attitudes have asked respondents to react to statements such as this:

> Where there is segregation, the Negro section should have the same equipment in paving, water, and electric-light facilities as are found in the white districts.

They are asked to record their opinions on a scale* designed as follows:

| (5) | (4) | (3) | (2) | (1) |
|---|---|---|---|---|
| Strongly approve | Approve | Undecided | Disapprove | Strongly disapprove |

*Likert* scales (1932) are of this type.

While questionnaire scales are the most commonly used attitude-measuring devices, other means have been used to measure the positiveness of a subject's attitude toward another person. Many investigators prefer to use an index of attitude which can be collected more naturally than can questionnaire measures. They fear that when a subject is forced to consider what his own attitudes are, his introspection may cause him to change his attitude in the process of describing it. Webb, Campbell, Schwartz, and Sechrest (1966), in a delightful book, discuss several indirect techniques, described below, which can be and have been used to measure one person's attraction for another.

*Tests of opinion disguised as tests of facts.* What a person assumes to be the "facts of the matter" often seems to be dependent on his attitudes. Members of the John Birch Society are undoubtedly less likely to read the *Daily Worker* than are members of the Communist Party, and thus they are less likely ever to be exposed to factual material favoring the Soviet Union. Further, even if John Birchers are exposed to pro-Communist facts, they are probably more likely to forget or to distort them than are Communists. The same selective exposure to facts and selective remembering of facts operates in all groups; Communists would also be expected to forget or distort information supporting the John Birch position. The notion that one tends to forget what he doesn't like to remember has been supported by

Levine and Murphy (1943), Edwards (1941), Watson and Hartman (1939), Weiss (1953) and Taft (1954).

Some experimenters have taken advantage of this correlation between factual information and positiveness of attitudes as an indirect way of measuring attitudes (Loeblowitz-Lennard and Riessman, 1946, Newcomb, 1946, Parrish, 1948, Hammond, 1948, and Cattell, *et al.,* 1950). By the "error-choice" technique, Hammond, for example, measured attitudes toward labor and management. The respondent was requested to choose between two alternative answers, each of which was equally wrong, but wrong in opposite directions from the correct answer. One erroneous answer favored labor, the other management. It was assumed that the direction one's errors took indicated the side one favored.

*Eye-contact.* When two people are engaged in conversation, they look one another in the eye intermittently and for short periods. Argyle (1967) found that the amount of time individuals look at one another varies from 30 percent to 60 percent. One determinant of how long individuals gaze at one another appears to be interpersonal attraction. The frequency of glances has been found to correlate positively with an individual's liking for another, and with the extent to which he desires to initiate or maintain his interaction with the other.

*Pupil size.* Hess and Polt (1960) proposed that pupil size also may serve as an index of attraction. An incident suggested to Hess that one's pupils might dilate when he observed especially interesting or pleasurable stimuli. Hess (1965) quickly checked this hypothesis in an informal experiment with a graduate student.

> When my assistant, James M. Polt, came in, I made him the subject of a quick experiment. I shuffled the pictures and, holding them above my eyes where I could not see them, showed them to Polt one at a time and watched his eyes as he looked at them. When I displayed the seventh picture, I noted a distinct increase in the size of his pupils; I checked the picture, and of course it was the pin-up he had been looking at. Polt and I then embarked on an investigation of the relation between pupil size and mental activity.*

Apparently, Hess was not the first to observe a correlation between pupil size and attraction. Hess (1965) discovered that Chinese jade dealers have long known that they could gain valuable information by carefully

---

*Hess, E. H. "Attitude and pupil size," reprinted by permission of *Scientific American;* 1965, **212**, p. 46.

observing a buyer's eyes. Such scrutiny presumably helps the seller guess when the buyer is impressed by a specimen and is likely to pay a high price. Subsequent research by Hess and his colleagues provides tentative evidence that pupil size may indeed be a valuable index of how attractive one finds various visual images.

*The distance one stands from another.* Members of different nationalities habitually stand different distances apart from one another when conversing. South Americans, for example, normally stand much closer together when conversing than do Americans. How far away from another it is "correct" to stand is an unconscious norm; adjustment to the correct distance is made automatically by the participants. When members of different cultural groups get together to talk, the unconscious norm as to how far apart individuals should stand often becomes a source of awkwardness. For example, in a mixed group of North Americans and South Americans, the South American is likely to keep moving forward to attain the "proper" speaking distance while the American keeps backing up to attain a more comfortable distance. On one occasion, we observed a South American colleague moving forward as he conversed, while his American counterpart moved steadily backward, down the entire length of a corridor. The American finally ended up pinned against a file cabinet at the end of the corridor, while the South American had finally attained the speaking distance that was comfortable for him.

As well as cultural differences in how close it is proper to stand, there seems to be intra-individual variability in how close one stands to others. In general, we seem to stand slightly closer to those we like than to those we abhor. In their research, Goldberg, Kiesler, and Collins (in press) and Kiesler and Goldberg (1968) have utilized standing distance as a measure of liking.

Other measures of interpersonal attraction that have been considered include:

*Favor-doing.* Bramel (1969) has noted "If we truly like someone, it pleases us to see him happy and hurts us to see him suffer. If we dislike him, our reaction is just the opposite. If this is so, then the person should be expected to give to those he likes the things he believes they want, and those he dislikes the things he believes they do not want." The extent to which a person will exert himself to provide benefits for others has been utilized as a measure of liking in several experiments.

*Sociometric choices.* It is generally assumed that the more we like someone, the more anxious we will be to associate with him. Thus one's choices as to whom he will associate with have been used as measures of liking in several experiments.

A sociometric test is a means of obtaining quantitative data on the preferences of group members for associating with other members (cf. Moreno, 1934). In this test, an individual may be asked to choose whom he wants most or least as a roommate or as a seatmate, etc.

From the preceding discussion it is clear that a great variety of measures have been conceived to indicate how much "attraction" one feels toward another. Whether the experimenter is using an attitude measure, a sociometric choice, or frequency of eye contact, the experimenter feels he is measuring a single variable—interpersonal attraction.

# CHAPTER TWO

# The Effect of Accidental Consequences on Liking

When we attempt to explain why we are attracted to a friend or repulsed by an enemy, we inevitably cite some characteristics of that person—his appearance, his personality, his humanity—as the explanation for our feelings. There is evidence, however, that there are two potent determinants of one's liking for another which have nothing to do with the other's characteristics.

In this chapter we will see evidence that things which happen to another, even when these events are beyond the other's control, may have a large effect on our own attitudes toward him. We will also see that the way in which we treat another person may profoundly affect our subsequent attitudes toward him. We often come to dislike people we exploit and like people we benefit, as well as the other way around.

## THE EFFECT OF CHANCE CONSEQUENCES

There are two popular sayings—"Nothing succeeds like success" and "Everybody loves a winner." Is it true that we like those who have for- tuitously succeeded and dislike those who have accidentally failed? If so, why should that be?

One reason we praise or blame others for the accidental consequences they encounter may simply be that we automatically assume that people get what they deserve. Since we know that many of the things that happen to people are in some way a consequence of their own actions, our best guess in an ambiguous situation is that the person is probably at least partially responsible for his fate. When someone admits to us that everyone is out to get him, and that all his attempts to improve his lot are blocked by a malevolent fate, we become suspicious. We usually reject the possibility that, through no fault of his own, the last 270 people he met just happened to be sadists. It is possible that an individual would have such a run of bad luck, but it is so unlikely that we do not really seriously consider the possibility.

There is evidence, however, that in many cases one's assumption that "people get what they deserve" may also be motivated by his desire to have the world seem to be a predictable place.

Walster (1966) proposed that when individuals hear about an accident, they will desire to blame someone (preferably the victim) for the accident. The desire to assign responsibility was assumed to increase as the consequences of the accident became increasingly serious. Walster argued that when one hears that someone has suffered a very small loss, it is easy to feel sympathy for him, to ascribe his misfortune to chance, and to acknowledge that unpleasant things can happen to a person through no fault of his own. As the magnitude of the misfortune increases, however, it becomes more and more unpleasant to acknowledge that "this is the kind of thing that could happen to anyone." Such an admission implies that a serious catastrophe could happen to oneself. If one can convince himself that the serious accident was the victim's fault, it is reassuring. Then one simply needs to assure himself that he is a different kind of person from the victim, or that he would behave differently under the circumstances which produced the accident, and he can then feel protected from catastrophe.

Walster tested this hypothesis by describing a youth's driving habits to groups of judges. In her description, she varied the degree of seriousness of the accident which was said to have resulted from the same pre-accident behavior. Her findings showed that the more serious the consequences were said to be, the more "morally unacceptable" the boy's behavior was judged to be and the more responsible he was considered to be for this accident.

Lerner and his associates conducted several experiments to test the hypothesis that people need to believe in a just world and will distort reality in order to maintain the belief that such a world does in fact exist. Lerner (1965) reasons that a belief in a just world is a prerequisite for survival. He says, "if people did not believe they could get what they want and avoid what they abhor by performing certain appropriate acts, they would be virtually incapacitated. It seems obvious that most people cannot afford, for the sake of their own sanity, to believe in a world governed by a schedule of random reinforcements."

There is considerable support for the proposal that observers will convince themselves that chance occurrences to others were actually deserved. Lerner (1965) had subjects observe two people working together at a task. They were told at the outset that one of the two workers would be selected *by chance* to receive a sizable amount of money for his efforts whereas the other worker would get nothing. In spite of the information that reward was randomly given, once the outcome was known to the observers they tended to persuade themselves that the person who had been awarded the money by chance really had earned it after all.

Many of Lerner's experiments utilize the following paradigm: Subjects gather in a waiting room a few minutes before the scheduled experiment and are joined by a confederate (the "victim"), who is a girl of their own age. The subjects then learn that they are to take part in a study on the perception of emotional cues, while the victim is to take part in a different study, a study on human learning, with another experimenter and in another room. They discover that in the learning study the other will be punished by receiving an electric shock every time she makes an incorrect response. The experimenter explains that the subjects are to judge the victim's emotional state while she is participating in the learning experiment. The subjects expect that they will view the victim's performance via a television monitor. Actually, subjects watch not a live closed-circuit television performance, as they expect, but a standard videotape. In all conditions the subjects see the same videotape. All subjects watch the victim receive several apparently painful electric shocks for her incorrect responses and they see the victim react to the shocks with expressions of pain and suffering. Then the subjects are asked to describe their reactions to the victim. This basic design has been used to test several hypotheses.

Lerner and Simmons (1966) suggest there are two ways in which one can convince himself that the world is indeed a just place, when faced with the fact that the innocent victim has been injured (shocked):

1.   he can convince himself that the victim deserved to suffer because she did not behave in an "appropriate or commendable fashion"; or

2.   he can convince himself that the victim deserved to suffer because she is an undesirable individual.

Lerner and Simmons first hypothesized that an observer would feel more compelled to justify the victim's suffering, and thus would derogate her more, when he believed that her suffering would continue, than if he believed that her suffering was at an end (or had occurred in the past). The authors varied the preceding design slightly to test this notion. They led one group of subjects to believe that the videotape they saw represented only the first half of an experiment; ostensibly, the victim was going to continue to be shocked even after the subject had completed his ratings. In other conditions, the videotape was said to represent the complete experiment. In still other conditions, the videotape was said to have been made some time ago. The authors' hypothesis was supported: There was more derogation of the victim when her suffering was only half over than when it was at an end or when the videotape was acknowledged to be several months old.

The authors' second hypothesis is the more surprising. Most of us would assume that people will admire and feel compassion for a person who has suffered for the sake of others—a person who is a martyr. For example, the sympathy Roman observers felt when observing the suffering of the Christian martyrs is often assumed to have encouraged the spread of Christianity. However, Lerner and Simmons point out that the suffering of someone who has acted out of altruistic motives should be extremely threatening to one's belief in a just world. A martyr, by virtue of his goodness, does not deserve to suffer. Thus, according to the authors' hypothesis, an observer should reject the willing martyr even more than he rejects the innocent victim.

This hypothesis was tested by altering the preceding experimental paradigm slightly. In the martyr condition, the victim claimed that she was afraid of electric shock and did not want to participate in the experiment. At the experimenter's urging she agreed to go on so that the observers could observe her and thereby satisfy a course requirement. The martyr was evaluated as less attractive than was a victim who had not expressed a fear of shock and then agreed to go on in order to help others.

### THE EFFECT OF TREATING ANOTHER UNJUSTLY

Recently a great deal of research has focused on the way in which one's treatment of another person will effect his subsequent liking for that person. Since the major portion of the research on this topic was designed to test various derivations from Festinger's theory of cognitive dissonance (1957), we must first discuss dissonance theory.

#### *Theory of Cognitive Dissonance*

The basic unit with which the theory works is the "cognition." "Cognition" is simply a shortened way of indicating "any knowledge, opinion, or belief about the environment, about oneself, or about one's behavior" that a person might hold.

Dissonance theory is concerned with the relationship that an individual's ideas have with one another. The theory states that three types of cognitive relationships are possible: dissonance, consonance, or irrelevance.

Cognitions are said to be in a *dissonant* relationship whenever they are incompatible (in Festinger's terminology when "the obverse of one element would follow from the other"). Cognitions can be dissonant for several reasons: Two cognitions can be incompatible because they contradict one another on logical grounds in the individual's own thinking system. For example, if a person believes that there is no such thing as a bad boy, and at the same time believes that a criminal character is hereditary, he should experience dissonance. Cognitions can also be dissonant because they oppose one's past experience about the necessary relationship between things. For example, suppose a climber slipped and fell at the summit of a mountain. If as he was falling he noticed that the trees below him were receding further and further in the distance, he should experience dissonance (as well as relief).

Cognitive elements are in a *consonant* relationship if one element follows from another on logical or experiential grounds.

Finally, cognitions can be in a totally *irrelevant* relationship to one another. For example, the cognitions "Englishmen are very proud of their gardens" and "Hotel rooms never have enough coat hangers" would probably be judged by nearly everyone to be totally irrelevant to one another.

Now that we have discovered how to go about classifying cognitions as dissonant, consonant, or irrelevant in their relationships, we can predict what will happen when the relationships are of various types. According to dissonance theory, the presence of dissonance gives rise to pressures to reduce or eliminate that dissonance and to avoid the increase of dissonance. In addition, the theory states that the more dissonance one is experiencing, the more anxious he will be to reduce his existing dissonance.

Researchers interested in interpersonal relations quickly saw and tested the implications of dissonance theory for interpersonal attraction. On the basis of the theory, they hypothesized that if an experimenter persuades individuals to behave in a cruel way, or in a very generous way, toward a neutral stranger, these individuals should tend to change their attitude toward the stranger so that it will be consistent with their behavior. If a subject harms another, he would be expected to justify his actions and thus come to dislike the person he has harmed. If the subject does a favor for another, he would be expected to convince himself that the other deserves his kindness and thus to increase his liking for the other. Researchers also hypothesized that the more choice an individual feels he has about whether to treat the other person harshly or generously, the more he will tend to like a person he benefits and to dislike a person he harms.

Let us now consider data relevant to these hypotheses.

*Evidence that an exploiter will justify his harm-doing.* One way an individual can reduce the dissonance he feels at injuring another who obviously does not deserve such treatment is by convincing himself that there is actually justification for his behavior. That individuals often justify their cruelties was apparent even to the ancients. Tacitus argued, "It is a principle of human nature to hate those whom you have injured." Derogation of the victim is, of course, only one way by which a harm-doer can justify his harm-doing. He can also justify his exploitation by minimizing the victim's suffering, by denying that he is responsible for the victim's suffering, or by insisting that the victim deserved to suffer.

One of the first experiments in this area was conducted by Davis and Jones (1960). These authors reasoned that since most individuals think of themselves as kind and fair persons, if they are led to injure another person, they should experience dissonance. One way the harm-doer can reduce his dissonance is by convincing himself that the victim deserved to suffer. Davis and Jones also argued that one's dissonance, and his tendency to reduce that dissonance, should increase as the choice he felt he had had about whether or not to harm the victim was increased.

In addition, the authors were interested in the fact that in naturalistic situations an individual can sometimes "withdraw" or take back cruel behavior. For example, an individual who has insulted another person can say "I didn't mean it" or "I was playing a joke" and thereby partially eliminate the harm he has done. The authors hypothesized that when such "taking back" was possible, derogation of the victim would not occur.

To test these hypotheses, the authors ran an experiment in which subjects were led to give another person a very cruel evaluation of his personality. Half of the subjects (the Choice subjects) were cajoled into *volunteering* to read the negative evaluation to the stimulus person. The remaining subjects (the No-Choice subjects) were *forced* to read that negative evaluation. Whether or not subjects anticipated being able to withdraw their harsh criticism of the other was also varied. Half of the subjects (those in the Anticipation condition) expected to meet the other person later in the experiment, when it would be explained that the subject didn't really mean the harsh evaluation. The remaining subjects (those in the Non-Anticipation condition) were led to believe that a subsequent meeting was impossible and that the stimulus person would not be disabused.

The experimental requirements were implemented in the following way. When students appeared, they were told that they were taking part in an experiment on first-impression formation. Their main task was presumably to form a first impression of a person in an adjoining room. While the student listened, the experimenter interviewed the other person. The interviewee was actually a confederate who attempted to answer all questions in a friendly way. He seemed slightly nervous and quite involved in creating a favorable yet honest impression of himself. When the interview was over the experimenter asked the subject to rate the confederate. This evaluation constituted the pre-measure of the subject's attitude toward the victim.

At this point the experimenter manipulated his independent variables. He explained to the student that he was also interested in how people respond to extremely flattering or extremely negative evaluations of themselves. He then showed the student two prepared evaluations. One was complimentary; it contained such statements as "You sound like one of the most interesting persons that I have met since I came to Duke; I would really like to get to know you better." The other evaluation was negative; it contained statements such as "My over-all impression was not too favorable" and "I wouldn't go out of my way to get to know you." The experimenter explained that the subject should read one of these evaluations to the other person so that they could observe how he would react to the flattering or disparaging evaluation. If the subject had been randomly assigned to the Choice condition, the experimenter told him that he could choose either evaluation to read to the other student, but that he would appreciate it if he would choose the negative one. (This request was effective in getting nearly all subjects to agree to read the negative evaluation.) If the subject had been assigned to the No-Choice condition, he was simply told to read the negative evaluation.

If the subject had been assigned to the Anticipation-of-Interaction condition, the experimenter said that after they studied the other's reaction to the negative evaluation, he would explain to him that this was not the subject's true opinion. If the subject had been assigned to a Non-Anticipation-of-Interaction condition, the experimenter said that the subject would not be able to tell the other student that the negative evaluation did not represent a true opinion.

The negative evaluation which the students read to the interviewee was very harsh. It said:

> I hope that what I say won't cause any hard feelings, but I'll have to say right away that my over-all impression was not too favorable. To put it simply, I wouldn't go out of my way to get to know you. Maybe I'd change my mind if we could talk together in more natural surroundings, but from the way you speak—not so much what you said but how you said it—I'd guess that you'd have some personal problems that it would make it hard for us to get along very well. Your general interests, and so on, just strike me as those of a pretty shallow person.
>
> To be more specific: Frankly, I just wouldn't know how much I could trust you as a friend after hearing your answers to those moral questions. You took the easy way out every time. I guess I should point out that some of the things you said made a good impression on me, but that would be kind of a waste of time, since the general impression that I have is not too good. That's all I have to say.

After the subject read the negative evaluation, the experimenter asked the subject to rate the victim's likability, warmth, conceit, intelligence, and adjustment.

The dependent variable in which we are interested is the extent to which subjects' liking for the other changed from the pre-measure to the post-measure. These scores are presented in Table 2.1. Davis and Jones expected Choice subjects to derogate the victim more than No-choice subjects, and those in the Non-Anticipation-of-Interaction condition to derogate the victim more than Anticipation subjects. Thus, "Choice-Non-Anticipation" subjects should derogate the victim the most; "No-choice-Anticipation" subjects should derogate him the least.

It is clear from inspecting Table 2.1 that only the first portion of this hypothesis was confirmed. It is somewhat surprising to note that the No-choice-Anticipation condition, expected to produce the least dissonance,

TABLE 2.1
*Mean Before and Change Scores of
Summary Rating Evaluation*

| | Condition | | | |
|---|---|---|---|---|
| | Choice | | No Choice | |
| | Antic. | Nonantic. | Antic. | Nonantic. |
| Before[a] | | | | |
| M | 51.0 | 55.5 | 48.0 | 54.7 |
| Change[b] | | | | |
| M | −1.8 | −7.7[c] | −2.2 | −1.7 |

*Note.* The lower the Before score the more favorable the rating. A negative change score indicates change toward a less favorable impression.
$N = 10$ for each cell; total $N = 40$.
[a]F betw/with = .641.
[b]F betw/with = 3.41,/3 and 36 *df, p* < .05.
[c]Individual mean comparisons with C-Na (Choice- Nonanticipation)–NC-Na: $t = 3.222$, 19 *df, p* < .01; C-A: $t = 2.278$, 19 *df, p* < .05; NC-A: $t = 2.413$, 19 *df, p* < .05.

is very similar to the two moderate dissonance conditions. Apparently, whether or not one has any freedom to read the negative evaluation is not related to the production of dissonance as long as the subject feels he can retract his behavior in a subsequent meeting.

On the basis of this evidence, the authors concluded that in order for an individual to derogate his victim he must: (a) feel that he had some freedom not to behave in the unjust manner, and (b) realize that he cannot easily disclaim the behavior in the eyes of the target person. This experiment was replicated by Davidson (1964).

Glass (1964) has added to our understanding of the derogation process. He hypothesized that the higher the harm-doer's own self-esteem, the more likely he will be to derogate someone he victimizes. Glass points out that if one believes that he has a preponderance of unfavorable characteristics, the knowledge that he has injured another should not be especially dissonance-arousing. It is true that he has behaved in a socially disapproved way; however, his cruel act is consonant with his general low self-regard. When one believes he is a fine, kind, intelligent person, however, knowledge of his aggression causes both a serious conflict with social norms *and* with his self-image. Thus, Glass concludes, the higher one's self-esteem, the more he should be motivated to explain away his cruel behavior by derogating the victim.

To test this hypothesis, Glass utilized a 2 × 2 design. Two weeks before the experimental session, the students took a series of psychological tests. The results of these tests were returned to subjects at the beginning of the experimental session. Unknown to the subjects, the results each received had been falsified. Actually, only two personality reports were given out, one favorable and the other unfavorable. By this procedure Glass hoped to increase the self-esteem of half of his subjects and to decrease the self-esteem of the remainder. If the subject's report was designed to raise his self-esteem, he was told that the test results had revealed that he was personable, mature, mentally alert, intelligent, and that he had a concern for the feelings of others. If his report was designed to lower his self-esteem, he **was** said to have received a poor score on the preceding characteristics.

After the bogus personality report had been returned to the subject, he **and** a confederate worked together on a concept-formation task. The student was asked to be the "experimenter," the confederate to be the "subject" in the task. Each time his partner made an error, the student was to administer a 100-volt shock to the "subject." Half of the subjects (Choice condition subjects) were given the option of refusing to administer a series of seemingly painful electric shocks to the other person. Half of the subjects (No-Choice condition) were simply directed to administer the electric shocks.

The concept-formation task consisted of 60 "learning" trials. The confederate pretended to make 24 incorrect responses. Each time the student punished him for his error, the confederate gasped and moved in discomfort in order to lead the student to believe that he was causing the confederate considerable pain. When the learning trials were complete, the student was asked to indicate his liking for the victim. Students were also asked about their attitudes toward the use of electric shock in experiments and asked to estimate the painfulness of the shocks they had administered to the confederate. Glass's hypothesis was confirmed. There was a significant interaction between the choice and self-esteem treatments: When they had had a choice about whether or not to harm the victim, harm-doers who possessed high self-esteem did derogate the victim; those with low self-esteem did not. When subjects were *forced* to harm the victim, no derogation occurred in either self-esteem condition.

Researchers have also shown that one can reduce the dissonance he experiences at injuring another by two additional techniques: (1) he can minimize the victim's suffering, or (2) he can attempt to deny responsibility for the victimization.

Brock and Buss (1962 and 1964) investigated the latter justification techniques. In what was presumably a learning experiment, they required their subjects to teach another subject a concept and to shock him whenever he made an incorrect response. The independent variables which the authors considered in their experiments were: the degree of choice given to the subject about whether or not to shock the victim, the amount of justification he was given for acting as a supervisor, the amount of shock he was to administer to the victim, the extent to which he was allowed to communicate with the victim, and the sex of the subject and of his victim. The dependent variables the authors utilized were: How much obligation the subject said he felt to shock the victim, how painful he perceived the shocks delivered to the victim to be, and the extent to which he justified the use of shock in experiments. The authors' results are extremely multitudinous and too complex to allow more than a few of their findings to be summarized here.

Brock and Buss (1962) found that when subjects were allowed to choose whether or not to administer shock, they minimized the painfulness of the shocks they delivered more than did subjects who were forced to shock the victim. (In fact, those subjects who were forced to administer shocks exaggerated the painfulness of the shocks they were required to administer.) Lerner and Matthews (1967) found that the more responsible one felt for the victim's suffering, the more he derogated him. These findings are consistent with the notion that the more responsible an individual feels for another's suffering, the more compelled he will feel to justify his own unjust behavior.

In addition, Brock and Buss found that individuals who were asked to give high shocks to the victim reported that they felt more obligated to administer shock, than did subjects who were asked to give lower shocks. (The experimenter's request was phrased exactly the same, regardless of the amount of shock the subject was asked to deliver.) Brock and Buss (1964) replicated this finding. Lerner and Simmons (1966) also found that the more harm done to a victim, the more the harm-doer would derogate him. This evidence seems to provide additional support for the notion that the more harm an individual does, the more anxious he will be to justify his behavior in some way.

*Evidence that an exploiter will make restitution to the exploited.* It has not often been observed that it is a principle of human nature for the exploiter to make restitution to the exploited. Junius' cynical comment in his *Letters* that "A death bed repentance seldom reaches to restitution" is a common observation. In spite of the cynicism of philosophers, recent studies have verified the fact that one way an individual reacts to seeing another suffer is to make restitution to him.

That a harm-doer will attempt to compensate a victim has been demonstrated by Walster, Walster, Abrahams, and Brown (1966), Walster and Prestholdt (1966), Berscheid and Walster (1967), Freedman, Wallington, and Bless (1967), Carlsmith and Gross (in press), Berscheid, Walster, and Barclay (in preparation), and Berscheid, Boye, and Walster (in press).

## Compensation or Justification?

Operating from different theoretical positions, experimenters have proposed and demonstrated that harm-doers may react in three quite different ways to harming another: They may justify their harmful action, they may attempt to compensate the victim for the harm he has suffered, or they may punish themselves in some way for injuring the other. (This latter reaction seems to be a relatively unusual type of response. Reactions of this type are reported only in the clinical literature.)

Knowing when a harm-doer is likely to react to his harm-doing by compensating the victim or by justifying the victim's suffering is important. This is especially true since the two different possible reactions have diametrically opposed consequences for the victim. For example, when the harm-doer justifies the harm he has done, he denies responsibility for it, convinces himself that his behavior was acceptable, and presumably should be more willing to engage in the behavior a second time (Berscheid, Boye, and Darley, 1968). On the other hand, if the harm-doer decides to compensate the victim for his suffering, he accepts responsibility for his harm-doing, tries to make up for his unacceptable behavior, and presumably would be less willing to do the same thing again.

Several situational variables seem to determine whether or not a harm-doer responds to his victim with justice or with justification.

*Adequacy of available restitution.* By "adequacy of compensation" is meant the extent to which a compensation benefits the victim, relative to the harm done him. According to the definition, an available compensation may lack adequacy for two reasons: It is inadequate to cover the harm done, or it is an excessive restitution relative to the harm done.

Berscheid and Walster (1967) and Berscheid, Walster, and Barclay (in preparation) have shown that the more adequate a harm-doer perceives an available compensation to be, the greater is the probability that he will choose to restore equity by compensating the victim.

Although a victim would undoubtedly prefer an inadequate compensation to no compensation at all, from the harm-doer's point of view, making a partial compensation is an unsatisfactory way to restore equity. A partial compensation cannot by itself restore equity, since the victim is still left in a deprived state. Similarly, excessive compensation cannot, by itself, eliminate the harm-doer's distress. An excessive compensation eliminates one kind of inequity by producing another. There is evidence that individuals experience dissonance when they over-benefit another as well as when they deprive him of deserved benefits (Walster, and Prestholdt [1966], and Jecker and Landy [in press]).

For these reasons, it was predicted that individuals would be less likely to compensate their victims (and presumably more likely to justify the victim's suffering instead) when available compensations were inadequate or excessive than when they were adequate. Berscheid and Walster (1968) found support for this hypothesis in an experiment conducted with women's church groups.

In this experiment, women were led to cheat a fellow parishioner out of trading stamps in a vain attempt to win additional stamps for themselves.

(Interviews with pre-test subjects revealed that women felt quite guilty when they ruminated on their actions.) When the women were subsequently given an opportunity to compensate the victim, at no cost to themselves, it was found that adequacy of available compensation was of crucial importance in determining whether or not the women would choose to compensate. Women who could compensate with an adequate compensation, exactly replacing the number of books the partner had lost, were much more likely to compensate than were women limited to insufficient compensation (a few stamps) or to excessive compensation (a great many stamp books). In the control conditions (when women could only "compensate" a partner she had not injured) this tendency did not exist. This finding was replicated by Berscheid, Walster, and Barclay (in preparation).

If we accept these findings at face value, they have some surprising implications. In real life, opportunists often try to impress upon those in a position to make restitution how much they have suffered in the hope of eliciting as much restitution as possible. They naturally assume that the better a case one makes for his claim, the more likely it is that he will be compensated. The preceding research, however, indicates that in some instances, it might be more effective strategy for a victim to minimize his description of his suffering rather than to aggrandize it. Increasing the amount of debt claimed might be an effective way to secure increased benefits if the exploiter can conceivably make a restitution adequate to cover the suffering described. If, however, one aggrandizes his suffering to such an extent that it exceeds the highest level of compensation available to the exploiter, the victim would increase his chances of receiving no compensation at all, and perhaps of having his suffering justified instead.

*Anticipation of retaliation.* An exploiter's justification of his harmful act is potentially very dangerous. Not only does the harm-doer end up with a distorted and unreal assessment of his actions, but he may commit further acts based on his distorted perceptions (Berscheid, Boye, and Darley, 1968). This is likely to leave the victim in sad straits. Not only has he been hurt, but as a result of the harm-doer's justification, the probability that the harm-doer will hurt him again has been increased. Obviously, from the victim's point of view, it is desirable to have equity restored before the perpetrator is forced to justify what he has done. If the harm-doer is unable or unwilling to restore equity by making restitution, how may the victim prevent justification? In our culture the phrase "getting even" suggests that equity can be restored by the victim's retaliation against the harm-doer.

Berscheid, Boye, and Walster (in press) conducted an experiment designed to assess the effect that a victim's retaliation has on the exploiter's tendency to justify the victim's suffering. The measure of justification which they used was derogation of the victim.

In this experiment, individuals were hired to administer electric shocks to another person. After arriving at the experiment, half of the subjects were told that they were to shock a fellow student. The remainder of the subjects were told to observe the harm-doing; they were simply to be innocent bystanders. Immediately before the victim was injured, the experimenter led half of the harm-doers and half of the observers to anticipate that the victim would shock *them* at the conclusion of the experiment. The remaining harm-doers and observers were led to believe that they would not be shocked.

The authors proposed that subjects who shocked the victim but who were not going to be shocked in return would derogate the victim (as Davis and Jones, 1960, and Davidson, 1964, demonstrated they would.) They predicted, however, that those harm-doers who expected to be shocked by the victim in return would not need to derogate him, since by his retaliation he would restore equity to the harm-doer—victim relationship.

The data confirmed the authors' hypothesis. When a boy had himself harmed the victim, he liked the victim more (or derogated him less) when he expected retaliation than when he did not. This finding cannot be construed as simply a demonstration that we tend to like those who have power over us. The relationship between retaliation and liking was very different for the observers who merely observed the victim's suffering. Observers who expected to be hurt by the victim in the future liked him *less* than did those who did not expect to be hurt.

James Baldwin (1964) in a statement concerning the Negro's struggle for minority rights in this country, argues, "Neither civilized reason nor Christian love would cause any of those people to treat you as they presumably wanted to be treated; only *fear* of your power to retaliate would cause them to do that, or to seem to do it, which was (and is) good enough." Negro militants have taken an even stronger position. They argue that widespread Negro violence is necessary to restore the Negro to full citizenship. The variables they discuss sound much like those we have considered. They talk of the "White Devil," his guilt, his denial of racial injustices, and the equity-establishing effects of violence. If extrapolation from the preceding findings is relevant, we might suggest that retaliation, or the anticipation of retaliation, will be beneficial only if the recipient of the violence feels that he is in some way directly responsible for the Negro suffering: On the basis of the preceding data, retaliation against those who believe themselves to be innocent observers of injustice would seem to be a disastrous strategy.

*Public commitment.* In studies of attitude change, public commitment has been shown to be an important determinant of whether or not a person will be willing to admit error and to change his mind. Brehm and Cohen (1962) review several studies of this type. They find that if a person feels his views are well known to others, he is much more likely to resist changing his mind when faced with new evidence which contradicts his views, than if his initial opinions are unknown to others. There is evidence that this same principle operates in the area of interpersonal attraction.

Walster and Prestholdt (1966) conducted an experiment with social work trainees. They were told they would be working on an actual case, with actual clients. Ostensibly, the trainees' job was to listen to case histories in which different social workers discussed two clients—a daughter and her mother. It was the trainees' job to make a realistic, uninhibited, and accurate evaluation of each client.

Before the trainees heard the first social workers' reports, they were given some background information concerning the clients. Control group subjects were warned that the report which they would soon hear was not entirely correct, that certain events were misleading, and if taken at face value would lead one to make an overly generous evaluation of the mother and an overly harsh evaluation of her daughter. Experimental group subjects did not receive this warning.

Trainees then heard the first report, and wrote an evaluation of both clients and a recommendation as to the type of treatment they should receive. Control subjects, who had been warned to disregard certain false information, naturally wrote a fair evaluation of the clients. Experimental subjects, who had not received complete information, usually wrote an unjustly harsh evaluation of the daughter and an overly generous evaluation of the mother.

After completing their evaluations, the trainees were randomly assigned to be either strongly committed or uncommitted to their initial evaluations. Strongly committed subjects were required to sign their evaluations; their instructor read their evaluations and then sent them to the clients' psychiatrist. Uncommitted subjects were allowed to keep their evaluations; they were told they could simply rip them up and throw them away.

Trainees then heard the second case report, which argued that the first report was misleading and which presented information contradicting the impression of the clients provided in the first report. Finally, the experimenter asked the subjects to make a final and anonymous evaluation of the clients.

The data support the hypothesis that commitment is a crucial variable in determining whether a person will change his mind in the face of new information or will attempt to justify his unjust treatment and continue to treat the other unjustly. Committed trainees continued to adhere to their overly-harsh or overly-favorable evaluations long after receiving the correct information. Uncommitted trainees were quite willing to change their minds. (In fact, uncommitted subjects seemed to bend over backwards to be fair after their initial error. They were even more favorable to the daughter and more harsh to the mother than were control subjects.)

The authors were also interested in whether or not the predicted variations in liking would affect the trainees' attitude toward the client. Thus, immediately after the subjects had evaluated the clients for the last time, the instructor mentioned that social work volunteers were now needed to assist the clients described. Offers to help the various clients were consistent with the liking subjects expressed for them.

*Possible segregation from the victim.* It is probably true that one is more likely to justify the suffering of a victim he expects never to see again, than to justify the suffering of a victim with whom he anticipates subsequent contact. There are several reasons why it is more difficult to distort one's perception of an intimate than one's perception of a stranger.

First, Cartwright and Harary (1956), Festinger (1957), Abelson and Rosenberg (1958), Rosenberg (1960), and Zajonc (1960) have argued that it is more difficult to change a belief which is consistent with many other beliefs which an individual holds, than to change a belief which exists in isolation. The more intimate we are with someone, the more likely it is that we will have many consistent beliefs and attitudes toward him. Thus, distortion of an intimate's characteristics is less likely than distortion of a stranger's traits, since more beliefs need to be altered in order to produce a consistent attitude in the former case than in the latter. It may be easy enough to convince ourselves that a stranger deserved to be hurt; it is much more difficult to convince ourselves that the victim deserved to suffer if we know many good things about him which contradict our distortion.

Further, Walster, Berscheid, and Barclay (1967) demonstrated that one is less likely to engage in distortions when the distortions are likely to be challenged by future objective evidence than when they are not. If a person expects to continue to associate with the victim, it becomes very risky to distort his characteristics. If one engages in a massive distortion of an intimate's character, he must anticipate that it is inevitable that he will soon be embarrassingly confronted with the actual victim, who may demonstrate that he possesses traits quite different from those one had ascribed to him.

Finally, in any relationship, the more clearly one can perceive the characteristics and motives of those with whom he is going to interact, the greater are his chances of securing the positive outcomes he desires. Distortion of perception of an intimate would produce the anticipation of greater cost than would distortion toward a stranger and thus should be less likely to occur.

There is some data available to test this hypothesis. Davis and Jones (1960) found that subjects who expected to see their victim after delivering a cruel evaluation to him did not derogate him. Derogation did occur among subjects who did not anticipate any subsequent interaction with the victim.

These arguments suggest that familiarity should tend to breed accuracy and should discourage the use of justification as an equity-restoring technique (Kiesler and Kiesler (1969) also discuss this point). This hypothesis has certain implications. For example, so long as Negroes are geographically and socially segregated, individuals who exploit Negroes can conveniently reduce whatever distress they feel because of their exploitation, by derogating the exploited. It is easy for them to maintain that Negroes deserve their exploitation (e.g., "They are shiftless and lazy, and don't want a job.") or that they are not really suffering (e.g., "A Negro can live better on $1 than a white man can on $5"). Integrated housing and forced association would be expected to make utilization of such rationalizations very difficult.

## Aggrandizement of a Beneficiary

Until now we have concentrated entirely on how a harm-doer will respond to someone that he has unjustly injured. However, we are also interested in the opposite proposition. "How will an individual respond after conferring an undeserved benefit on someone?"

Several researchers have suggested that unmerited kindness produces dissonance in a benefactor. If a person has the cognition that people should get what they deserve, and only what they deserve, and yet he finds himself in the position of gratuitously rewarding an undeserving person, he will experience dissonance. One way to reduce this dissonance is to convince oneself that the recipient of the benefit is in fact more deserving than he had initially thought.

Gerard (1966) points out that Aristotle and Aquinas both believed that a benefactor comes to love the recipient of his favors. Both asked and attempted to decide "Whether a man ought to love more his benefactor than one he has benefited." The reasons they give for why one does love a person he benefits (while he tends to resent the person who has benefited *him*) sound surprisingly as if they had been reading dissonance theory. For example, Aristotle notes: ". . . it is more difficult to give than to receive favors: and we are most fond of things which have cost us most trouble, while we almost despise what comes easy to us."

The data supporting the hypothesis that doing a favor for someone produces liking for the recipient are consistent but weak. In several studies, the results have come out in the direction predicted, but have not reached acceptable levels of statistical significance.

Hastorf and Regan (personal communication) conducted a study in which a lame student asked another student to go over to pick up some pills that he needed at the Health Service. He claimed to be unable to get the pills himself. In some cases, the trip to the Health Service required the expenditure of a great deal of effort; the subject was required to walk there in the winter, in very poor weather. In other conditions, the trip was not so effortful; the weather was mild. Hastorf and Regan found that individuals who had to exert more effort to do the favor liked the recipient of their kindness better than did individuals who performed a less effortful favor. This difference, however, was not statistically significant.

In the Walster and Prestholdt (1966) study discussed earlier, social work trainees were led to give one of their clients an overly favorable evaluation. When individuals were publicly committed to this initial over-evaluation, they tended to justify their leniency, and to continue to overrate the client in subsequent evaluations. This over-evaluation continued in spite of continuing evidence that the client did not deserve such a kind rating. When trainees were not publicly committed to a lenient evaluation, or when their initial evaluation had been more moderate, this subsequent over-evaluation did not occur.

Jecker and Landy (in press) conducted a very ingenious experiment in this area. They proposed that if an individual expended his effort, time, or material possessions in order to benefit another person—especially if he disliked that person—he would experience dissonance. When one does not particularly like a person, and has no reason to suspect that the person will reciprocate a kindness, one has very little justification for performing a favor. The authors thought that if subjects were led to help someone they disliked, they would try to justify doing the undeserved favor by increasing their esteem for the other. They also proposed that the larger the favor one performed, the more dissonance he would experience, and the more he would increase his liking for the initially disliked other.

Their hypotheses were tested in the following way. Subjects were recruited to participate in a concept formation task. By design, they won either 60 cents or $3.00 at the task. Throughout the experiment, the experimenter behaved in a uniformly rude and brusk way towards them.

Subjects were randomly assigned either to a No-Favor condition, to the FE condition (a condition in which they did a favor for the experimenter), or to the FP condition (a condition in which they did a favor for someone other than the experimenter). If the subject had been assigned to the FE condition, the experimenter said to him "I wonder if you could do me a favor. The funds for this experiment have run out and I'm using my own money to finish the experiment. As a favor to me, would you mind returning the money you won?" If the subject hesitated, the experimenter said "I can't make you return the money, but I wish you would as a favor to me." After returning their money, the subjects reported to the departmental secretary. If the subject had been assigned to the No-Favor condition or to the FP condition, he reported directly to the departmental secretary.

When a subject turned in his slip to the secretary, the secretary noted whether or not the subject had been assigned to the FE condition. If the subject had already returned his winnings to the experimenter, the secretary simply gave him a questionnaire to fill out. The subjects were to evaluate various aspects of the experiment in which they had participated, ostensibly for the Psychology Department. Actually, this questionnaire constituted the dependent measure. As part of this questionnaire, subjects were asked to rate their personal liking for the experimenter.

Subjects who still had their winnings were treated in one of two ways. No-Favor subjects were also given the Psychology Department's question-naire as soon as they arrived. FP subjects were in a control treatment in which they were asked to do a favor for someone other than the experimenter. In this condition, the secretary said: "The money Mr. Boyd is using comes from the Psychology Department's research fund, which is running extremely low. The department would appreciate your doing it a favor by returning the money to the fund." After these subjects had returned their winnings, they filled out the dependent measure.

The results of this experiment were as follows: As predicted, those subjects who returned the money to the experimenter liked him better than did the subjects who returned their money to the Psychology Department. The second hypothesis was that the bigger the favor one performed for the experimenter, the greater would be one's liking for him; subjects who returned $3.00 should have liked the experimenter better than subjects who returned only 60 cents. The differences in liking expressed by subjects in these conditions were in the predicted direction, but they were not statistically significant.

# CHAPTER THREE

# Rewards Others Provide: Reduction of Anxiety, Stress, Loneliness or Insecurity

### LIKING PRODUCED BY REWARDS OTHERS PROVIDE

The psychological principle which is most frequently used to predict interpersonal attraction is the principle of *reinforcement:* We will like those who reward us; we will dislike those who punish us. In this chapter and the four which follow we will discuss research relevant to this principle.

Several theorists have elaborated upon the relationship between reinforcement and interpersonal attraction. For example, Homans' (1961) theory rests largely on the general proposition that a necessary condition for receiving esteem from others is the capacity to reward them. He hypothesizes further that

> A man's esteem depends upon the relative rarity of the services he provides if we take a larger look at the ways in which a man may help others. If he has capacities of heart, mind, skill, experience, or even strength that they do not have, and uses these capacities to reward others, he will get esteem from them. But if his capacities are of a kind that they also possess, or if these capacities are widely available in the group, he will not get much esteem even if he uses them in such a way as to reward the others (p. 150).

In other words, there are, according to Homans, rewards and rewards—one who provides rewards which are in short supply is more likely to evoke attraction than one who provides rewards which are relatively common.

Homans considers the costs as well as the rewards one can incur in a relationship and introduces the concept of profit. Profit is simply defined as the *amount of reward* a person receives from an interaction *minus the cost* he incurs in that interaction. The amount of social approval, or esteem, one has for another is hypothesized to be a function of the profit one obtains from one's interactions with the other.

Thibaut and Kelley (1959) view a person's attraction to another as a function of the extent to which the person achieves, in interaction with the other, a reward-cost ratio in excess of some minimum level. This minimum level is defined as the *comparison level* (or CL). The CL, according to Thibaut and Kelley is:

> ... some modal or average value of all the outcomes known to the person (by virtue of personal or vicarious experience), each outcome weighted by its salience (or the degree to which it is instigated for the person at the moment). A person's CL depends not only upon outcomes which he has experienced or seen others experiencing but also upon which of these are actively stimulating to him—are obtruded on him, are vivid and perhaps implicitly rehearsed as he makes an evaluation of his circumstances (p. 81-82).*

According to these theorists, then, how much a person will be attracted to another depends upon whether the outcomes the person obtains from the other are above or below his CL: "If the outcomes in a given relationship surpass the CL, that relationship is regarded as a satisfactory one. And, to the degree the outcomes are supra-CL, the person may be said to be attracted to the relationship. If the outcomes endured are infra-CL, the person is dissatisfied and unhappy with the relationship (p. 81)."

Thibaut and Kelley make a distinction between the feeling of liking one may have for another person and the extent to which one is dependent upon that other. A person could conceivably continue to interact with another, even though he was dissatisfied with the relationship (the outcomes he obtained from the relationship were below his CL). To explain why a person would continue in an unsatisfactory relationship, Thibaut and Kelley invoke the concept of *comparison level for alternatives* (or CL alt). The CL alt presumably acts as a standard against which the person evaluates whether or not he wishes to remain in a relationship with another person, and is defined as "... the lowest level of outcomes a member will accept in the light of available alternative opportunities ... The height of the CL alt will depend mainly on the quality of the best of the member's available alternatives, that is, the reward-cost positions experienced or believed to exist in the most satisfactory of the other available relationships (p. 21-22)." Although an individual may not be attracted to another (his outcomes are below his CL), he may continue to interact with the other simply because no more desirable alternative is available (the outcomes he obtains in the relationship are above his CL alt).

Lott and Lott (1961), extending Hullian learning theory to apply to the

---

*Thibaut, J. W. and H. H. Kelley. *The Social Psychology of Groups.* New York: Wiley and Sons, 1959, 80-99.

case of interpersonal attraction, have reasoned that a person should come to like not only those who provide rewards, but also those who have nothing to do with providing rewards, but are merely physically present when the individual receives rewards. They have reasoned that, like any other response, response to a reward becomes conditioned to all discriminable stimuli present at the time of reinforcement; another person, of course, may be a discriminable stimulus.

To test whether or not one tends to like those who just happen to be present at the time one receives a reward, Lott and Lott formed three-member groups of children. Each group then played a game in which some members of the group were rewarded and other members were not. Following participation in the game sociometric tests were administered to the children. Specifically the children were asked which two children in the class they would choose to take with them on their next family vacation.

The results of this study indicated that children who had been rewarded chose members of their three-person groups (who were present at the time of reward) significantly more often than unrewarded children chose members of their three-person groups. Thus, Lott and Lott concluded that the reward of success in the game had been conditioned to the other members of the group and this led to increased esteem for these members. Results of this study were corroborated by a subsequent study conducted by James and Lott (1964).

While it is generally accepted that "we will like those who reward us and dislike those who punish us," we must note that this statement does not, to any great extent, increase predictability in the area of interpersonal attraction. We have no equation which will permit us to add up all the rewards a stimulus person will provide and balance them against the punishment which he will inflict and thus arrive at a total reward index which will tell us how much others will like him. A multitude of things may be rewarding or punishing to any individual at a given time. In addition, it is often the case that "one man's meat is another man's poison"; individuals differ in what they find to be rewarding or punishing.

Since it is so difficult to calculate what one individual at one point in time will find rewarding, researchers in interpersonal attraction have been led to consider which behaviors and events most people, most of the time, will find rewarding. By considering some of the specific behaviors that have been found to be rewarding or punishing to people in a number of different situations—behaviors which appear to be "transituational reinforcers"—some predictive insight into interpersonal attraction has been gained.

## ANXIETY

There is much evidence that when individuals feel anxious, afraid, lonely or unsure of themselves, the sheer presence of others is particularly rewarding. Try an experiment: Come to class a few minutes early on a regular school day. You will probably find that few of your classmates approach you. Then, some time when an exam is scheduled in one of your classes, arrive a few minutes early. You may be surprised to see the number of classmates who approach you with friendly remarks or joking comments. There is a good psychological explanation for the observation that students seem friendlier on days when an exam is scheduled than on days when one is not.

Schachter (1959) tested the hypothesis that anxiety conditions will lead to an increased affiliative tendency. He recruited college women to participate in an experiment. When they arrived in the experimental rooms, the experimenter claimed that his investigation was concerned with the effects of electric shock. The description of the shock experiment was designed to make some of the women highly anxious, while leaving the remainder of the women calm. Specifically, anxiety was produced in the following way:

> In the high-anxiety condition, the subjects . . . entered a room to find facing them a gentleman of serious mien, wearing horn-rimmed glasses, dressed in a white laboratory coat, stethoscope dribbling out of his pocket, behind him an array of formidable electrical junk. After a few preliminaries, the experimenter began: "Allow me to introduce myself. I am Dr. Gregor Zilstein of the Medical School's Departments of Neurology and Psychiatry. I have asked you all to come today in order to serve as subjects in an experiment concerned with the effects of electrical shock" (1959, p. 12-13).*

To make matters worse, the series of electric shocks the girls were to receive were described as extremely painful.

In the low-anxiety condition, both the setting and the description of the experiment were designed to avoid arousing anxiety in the subjects. There was no electrical apparatus in the experimental room. The experimenter explained that he was concerned with extremely mild electrical shocks that would not in any way be painful. The "shocks" were said to resemble more a tickle or a tingle than anything unpleasant.

Once some women had been made more anxious than others, Schachter could examine how anxiety affected their desire to be with other individuals. He assessed subjects' desire to affiliate in the following way. The experimenter claimed that there would be about a ten-minute delay while several pieces of equipment were secured. Subjects were told that during the ten-minute break they could wait in a private cubicle. These rooms were

---

*Schachter, S. *The Psychology of Affiliation.* Stanford, Calif: Stanford University Press, 1959.

said to be comfortable and spacious; they all contained armchairs and there were books and magazines in each room. The experimenter also commented that some of them might want to wait with other girls. If they preferred to wait with others, they were asked to let the experimenter know. He then passed out a sheet upon which the subject could indicate whether she preferred to wait alone, or with others, or had no preference at all.

Schachter found support for his hypothesis that anxious people will be especially inclined to seek the company of others (see Table 3.1). Sixty-three per cent of the subjects in the high-anxiety condition wanted to wait with other subjects. In the low-anxiety condition only thirty-three per cent of subjects wished to wait with others.

Schachter had also asked girls to indicate how *strongly* they desired to be alone or with others. They could give answers varying from "I very much prefer being alone" (scored $-2$) through "I don't care very much" (0) to "I very much prefer being together with others" (scored $+2$). As the column labeled "Over-all Intensity" in Table 3.1 indicates, these data also support the notion that affiliative desire increases with anxiety.

The finding that the anticipation of stress produces an increased desire to affiliate has been replicated by Gerard and Rabbie (1961), Sarnoff and Zimbardo (1961), Zimbardo and Formica (1963) and Darley and Aronson (1966).

While anxiety appears to increase an individual's need for affiliation, there is evidence that anxious individuals are selective about the others with whom they wish to affiliate. Anxious people apparently do not wish to be in the company of just any other person. Instead, anxious individuals seem to prefer to associate with people who are in a situation similar to their own.

Schachter bases this conclusion on a study which is similar in many ways to the experiment just described. Two groups of college women were

TABLE 3.1

*Relationship of Anxiety to the Affiliative Tendency*

| | No. Choosing | | | Over-all intensity |
| --- | --- | --- | --- | --- |
| | Together | Don't care | Alone | |
| High Anxiety | 20 | 9 | 3 | +.88 |
| Low Anxiety | 10 | 18 | 2 | +.35 |
| | $X^2$ Tog. *vs.* Dc + A = 5.27 | | | $t = 2.83$ |
| | $.02 < p < .05$ | | | $p < .01$ |

led to anticipate that they would soon be severely shocked. Then they were asked whether they preferred to wait alone or with others. How the "others" were described varied. In one condition girls were given a choice between waiting alone or waiting with some girls who were said to be taking part in the same experiment. In the other condition, girls were told they could either wait alone or with girls who were waiting to talk to their professors and advisors. Sixty per cent of the girls who had a chance to visit with similar others chose to spend their time in the company of others. Not one girl who was given the option of waiting with girls who were waiting to talk with their professors chose to wait with others. Scores on the "Over-all Intensity Scale" revealed the same results. Girls did not seem to be especially anxious to associate with other girls unless these other girls were in a situation similar to their own. Schachter notes that this finding puts a limitation on the old saw "Misery loves company." Perhaps misery doesn't love just any kind of company—only miserable company.

Once we accept the proposition that when individuals are anxious they have a special desire to affiliate with people in situations similar to their own, the question arises as to why this would be so.

Schachter considers several possibilities:

1. *Escape.* When one is in a stressful situation, perhaps he anticipates that talking to others in the same situation may help him figure out a way to avoid the pain altogether.

2. *Cognitive clarity.* There is some evidence that individuals in ambiguous or novel situations will desire to talk with knowledgable others in order to gain some understanding of an otherwise incomprehensible event. Since receiving severe shock in an experimental setting is probably unique in the subject's experience, perhaps anxious subjects desire to associate with others in order to find out if the others know any more about what is going on than they do.

3. *Direct anxiety reduction.* People often comfort and reassure one another. Perhaps highly anxious subjects choose to wait with others in the hope that the others will bolster their courage.

4. *Indirect anxiety reduction.* An effective device for reducing anxiety is to "get one's mind off one's troubles." People may be seen as more diverting than books or magazines. Perhaps subjects choose to wait with others in order to prevent themselves from thinking about the shock which will be forthcoming.

5. *Self-evaluation.* People often use other people in order to evaluate the reasonableness of their own emotions and feelings. In this novel and emotion-producing situation, an individual probably is not quite sure exactly how she should be reacting. (Should she be angry at the experimenter? Slightly apprehensive about the shock? Terrified?) Perhaps high-anxiety subjects seek out others in an attempt to appropriately label and identify their own feelings.

On the basis of his experimentation, Schachter concluded that two of these alternatives were probably operating: (1) direct anxiety reduction and (2) self-evaluation. Ingenious experiments by Gerard and Rabbie (1961) and Gerard (1963) also support the notion that the need for self-evaluation is one factor which predisposes anxious individuals to choose to wait with others. In spite of the fact some of the other factors have not yet been shown experimentally to predispose anxious individuals to associate with others, some of these other alternatives do sound plausible and may possibly be shown to be important in future research.

### Ordinal Position, Anxiety, and Affiliation

In examining his data Schachter uncovered a surprising result. First-born children seemed to respond differently than later-borns when they were placed in the high-anxiety condition. First-borns seemed both more anxiety-prone than later-borns and more desirous of associating with others when they were anxious than were later-borns.

In attempting to account for this finding, Schachter speculated about the ways in which the early experience of first-born and later-born children might differ. Schachter could conceive of two reasons why first-born individuals might learn, to a greater extent than other children, that when they were distressed other human beings could reduce their distress and thus should be sought out.

First, Schachter argued, a mother might be more responsive to the anxiety and distress of her first child than to the anxiety and distress of later children. She might "respond to more signals, respond more quickly, stay longer, and generally do a more effective all-round job of reducing anxiety with the first child than with later children." By the time subsequent children were born, a mother might well be more blasé and sophisticated about child rearing. Thus she would respond more slowly to the second child's every cry. By the time the fourth or fifth child arrived, a mother might be too worn out to care very much. For this reason, first-born children might come to associate the experience of anxiety with its reduction by affectionate humans to a much greater extent than would later-borns.

In addition, Schachter points out that younger children might have more threatening and anxiety-provoking persons in their immediate environment than do first-borns. Schachter comments that "by reputation at least, older children get their exercise by knocking the younger ones about." For this reason, first-borns might develop, to a greater extent than would later-borns, the expectation that others would provide comfort and support.

On the basis of such reasoning, Schachter developed the hypothesis that under anxiety-provoking conditions, first-born and only children would manifest stronger affiliative needs than would later-born children. A reanalysis of the data thus far discussed provides support for this notion. First and only children strongly preferred waiting with others in the high-anxiety condition, whereas later-born children did not. One cannot simply conclude that first-born children are more sociable in general than later-born children, since in the low-anxiety condition there were no differences between the choices of first-born and later-born children.

Schachter cites two possible reasons for this finding: First, it is possible that anxiety-provoking situations arouse considerably more anxiety and fear in early-born children than in later-born children. Second, even if all individuals are made equally (and highly) anxious, first and only borns might still choose to be together more often than later-born subjects; Schachter found support for both these possible interpretations. Fear-arousing situations seem to frighten first-borns more than later-borns, *and* even when later-borns are frightened to the same extent as first-borns, the first-borns are *still* more anxious to affiliate with others than are their later-born counterparts.

## STRESS

There is some evidence that individuals who are placed in a stressful situation show less severe physiological disturbance if other individuals are present than if they are not. Bovard (1959) developed an intriguing and compelling theory concerning the effect of social stimuli on an individual's physiological response to stress.

Bovard first presents data (from Selye, 1950) that noxious stimuli (physical stress) induce a systemic, nonspecific response in the vertebrate organism.

> This response involves release of adrenocorticotrophic hormone (ACTH) from the anterior pituitary and the consequent release of adrenal cortical hormones (cortisone, 17-hydroxycorticosterone) into the blood stream. Their effects are in general protein-catabolic, involving conversion of protein into glucose, and specifically include maintenance of blood-pressure and blood-sugar (glucose) levels under shock (p. 267).*

Psychological stress is also reported to produce a pituitary-adrenal response, stimulating carbohydrate metabolism and protein breakdown. Bovard notes, however, "The important difference between psychological and physical stress is that the former does not directly affect the body cells and, hence, must be mediated by the central nervous system" (p. 267).

There is serious question as to whether the organism's pituitary-adrenal response to psychological stress has survival value. Bovard reports that experiments by Bartlett and his colleagues (Bartlett, Bohr, Helmendach, Foster, and Miller, 1954; Bartlett, Helmendach, and Bohr, 1953; Bartlett, Helmendach, and Inman, 1954) showed that animals subjected to emotional

---

*Bovard, E. W. "The effects of social stimuli on the response to stress," *Psych. Rev.,* 1959, **66**, 267-277.

stress (restraint) *and* physical stress (extreme cold) maintained body temperature far less adequately than animals subjected to physical stress alone. Since the pituitary-adrenal response to phychological stress seems to be maladaptive, Bovard concludes that "the inhibition or dampening of the emotional-excitement component of the response to physical stress should have survival value for the organism" (p. 268).

Since psychological stress, unlike physical stress, must be mediated by the central nervous system, Bovard proposes a technique for preventing such stress from adversely affecting the organism. He suggests that the physical presence of other animals of the same species, particularly others with whom the stressed animal has previously interacted, during the period when the animal is enduring stress, will have a protective effect.

Bovard argues that the presence of a familiar animal in the same stressing situation "calls forth in the organism a 'competing response' which inhibits, masks, or screens the stress stimulus, such that the latter has a minimal effect." This "inhibiting effect" is said to be produced in the following ways:

> A number of recent studies . . . have suggested a reciprocal inhibitory effect between the posterior hypothalamus . . . and the anterior hypothalamus and parasympathetic centers . . . Stimulation of the latter region would appear to inhibit activity of the former . . .
>
> The simplest hypothesis to account for the observed phenomena at the human and animal levels is, therefore, that the presence of another member of the same species stimulates activity of the anterior hypothalamus and thus, as a byproduct, inhibits activity of the posterior hypothalamus and its centers mediating the neuroendocrine response to stress. Previous interaction with the other person or animal, as the case may be, could be assumed to accentuate this effect (p. 269).*

This hypothesis is supported by the finding of Back and Bogdonoff (1964) that small groups of strangers undergoing the physical stress of venipuncture and withdrawal of a blood sample together, show a higher resultant level of free fatty acids in their blood streams than do comparable groups of friends undergoing the same experience.

Since the free fatty acid level of the blood is a resultant of sympathetic autonomic activity, and a precursor to cholesterol formation, this experimental finding indicates that the presence of persons with whom one has previously interacted, such as a small group of friends, inhibits the posterior hypothalamic and hence the sympathetic autonomic response to stress.

Bovard cites a multitude of physiological measures which could be used to test the hypothesis that the presence of other individuals lowers the intensity of an animal's responses to the stress stimuli. Necessary experi-

---

*Ibid.*

ments to support Bovard's hypothesis have not yet been conducted. Bovard, however, cites several studies already in existence which provide suggestive evidence that he may be correct.

Several studies suggest that the small groups to which an individual belongs provide a great deal of support to him when he is under stress. For example, combat studies suggest that a small group (a platoon bomber crew) is very effective in sustaining members under severe battle stress (e.g., Mandlebaum, 1952).

How a person reacts to drugs is known to depend to a large extent on the setting in which he takes the drug. Staff members at Boston Psychopathic Hospital (1955) report that most individuals who tried LSD in the hospital setting experienced stressful psychotic reactions. According to their report, however, those who took LSD in a group situation had a more pleasant experience than did those who tried the chemical individually. The authors conclude that group participation relieved the tension associated with the stressful LSD experience.

Several animal studies suggest that the presence of other animals diminishes an animal's disturbance in a stressful situation. Arsenian (1943), Liddell (1950), Davitz and Mason (1955), Conger, Sawrey and Turrell (1957), and Mason (1960) support such a conclusion. The evidence that the presence of others may help eliminate an individual's discomfort when he is experiencing stress, provides an additional reason why individuals might learn to affiliate with others in stressful circumstances.

## SOCIAL ISOLATION

There is evidence that even when not under stressful conditions, people prefer a fair amount of contact with others to being alone for any length of time. The strength of the desire for social intercourse with others was dramatically demonstrated by the results of a social reform experiment conducted in the early 19th century.

At this time one of the great prison architects was John Haviland. As the result of the Quakers' religious beliefs and the upsurge of "humanitarianism," an attempt was made in 1821 to reform the prison system. Haviland was commissioned to build a "perfect" and "humanitarian" prison. The Quaker reformers noticed that mingling among prison inmates produced strong friendships among the inmates which caused them to continue their friendships after being released. Such friendships among ex-criminals tended to lead ex-criminals back into a life of crime. In the humanitarian reformation, it was decided to prevent contact among the prisoners. It was thought that total social isolation would prevent harmful corruption, protect the criminal's good resolutions, and give him ample opportunity to ponder on his mistakes and make his peace with God. Haviland's architectural design, which provided for solitary confinement day and night, was extremely popular with prison commissioners and a great many prisons imitated this style. The wardens, however, soon found that great ingenuity had to be adopted to prevent prisoners from talking. For example, new ventilation systems had to be designed, for prisoners soon found that the regular systems could be utilized for purposes of communication.

Ultimately the policy of social isolation was found to produce undesirable results. The fact that many inmates became physically and mentally ill as a result of their solitary confinement and their lack of work eventually forced a change of policy. Current psychological knowledge would have enabled us to foresee this outcome.

By early childhood a person has usually developed a need for the company of people. Complete social isolation for any prolonged period of time is known to be a painful experience. "Cabin fever" is a familiar expression which epitomizes the discomfort that even brief social isolation brings. Schachter points out that the autobiographical reports of religious hermits, prisoners of war, and castaways make it clear that isolation is devastating (1959, p. 6).

He notes that three trends have been found to characterize the experience of individuals enduring absolute social deprivation.

1. The reported pain of the isolation experience seems typically to bear a nonmonotonic relationship to time. Pain increases to a maximum in many cases and then decreases sharply. This decrease in pain is frequently marked by onset of the state of apathy, sometimes so severe as to resemble a schizophrenic state of withdrawal and detachment.

2. There seems to be a stronger tendency for those in isolation to think, dream, and occasionally to hallucinate about people.

3. Those isolates who are able to keep themselves occupied with distracting activities appear to suffer less and to be less prone to develop apathy.

The data support the conclusion that complete social isolation is more unpleasant than normal human contact. It is evident that others provide some reward by their sheer physical presence; they stave off loneliness.

## INSECURITY

What effect does an individual's self-esteem have on his reaction to accepting or rejecting others? Clinicians seem to agree that a high self-esteem person is more receptive to another's love than is an individual with lower self-esteem. For example, Rogers (1951) says that the person who accepts himself will have better interpersonal relations with others.

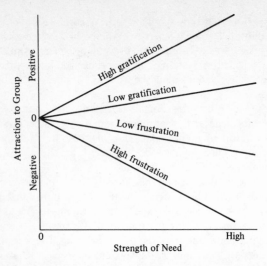

Fig. 3.1. Theoretical representation of attraction to a group as a function of the levels of a particular need of an individual and of the gratification of the need by the group

Adler (1926) adds that those who themselves feel inferior depreciate others. Horney (1939) views love as a capacity; she sees love of self and love of others as positively related. Fromm (1939), too, agrees with this notion. Studies supporting a positive relationship between self-esteem and liking or acceptance for others are reported in Berger (1952), Maslow (1942), Omwake (1954), and Stock (1949). These studies support the authors' contention that there is a positive relationship between self-esteem and liking.

A different prediction was made by Dittes (1959). He hypothesized that approval from other people would be especially rewarding to individuals low in self-esteem. He argued that:

> A person's attraction towards membership in a group, like motivational attraction toward any object, may be considered a function of two interacting determinants: (a) the extent to which his particular needs are satisfied by the group, and (b) the strength of his needs.*

Dittes assumed that the lower the level of one's own self-esteem, the greater would be his need for such supports to self-esteem as are provided by acceptance in a group. From this assumption, Dittes' predictions, which are diagramed in Fig. 3.1, can be clearly derived: (1) When another person is accepting, he satisfies a greater need in a low self-esteem person than in a

---

*Dittes, J. E. "Attractiveness of group as function of self-esteem and acceptance by group," *J. Abn. Soc. Psych.*, 1959, **59**, 77-82.

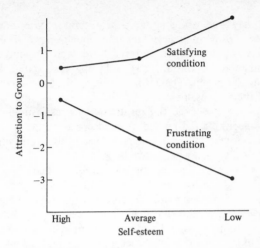

Fig. 3.2. Effects of acceptance and non-acceptance on attraction to group among persons with different levels of initial self-esteem.

high self-esteem person. Thus, acceptance should produce a greater increase in attraction the lower the self-esteem of the recipient. (2) When the other person is rejecting, he frustrates a greater need in the low self-esteem person than in the high self-esteem person. Thus rejection should decrease the other's attractiveness more, the lower the self-esteem of the recipient.

An experimental study provided support for Dittes' proposal. Subjects were college freshmen, who met in small groups of five or six members for a two-hour discussion task session. An attempt was made to make the group very attractive. During the first hour of discussion, the groups' conversation was interrupted three times to allow subjects to rate the desirability of having each of the other members in the group; these ratings were requested by the experimenter as though they were for his own interest. At an intermission, the subject's interest in these ratings was aroused and he was allowed to see privately what he believed to be the ratings of desirability made of him by other members of the group. Actually, the distributed ratings were fictitious, and had been prepared in advance to lead some subjects (those in the Satisfying condition) to believe that they were highly accepted by the group, and to lead others (those in the Frustrating condition) to believe that the group rejected them.

After some additional tasks had been performed, the subject's own attraction to the group was assessed. Individuals were asked if the group met again, how much would they like to continue working with it, how much they enjoyed participating in the experiment, and how disappointed would they be if not invited back to participate. Scores on these questions were summed to form an index of the subject's attraction to the group.

Dittes measured self-esteem in three ways: (1) Before the experimental session, subjects completed a self-esteem questionnaire. (2) At the end of the session, they were asked about their general sense of adequacy among groups of peers. (Since the acceptance manipulation would be expected to affect answers to this question, subjects' scores were computed separately in each experimental condition.) (3) Subjects were rated by the other individuals in the group. The ratings they received were considered to be indicative of their own self-esteem.

In Fig. 3.2, we can see the results that Dittes secured. The extent to which the subject believed he had been accepted by the group had a much greater effect on whether or not he reciprocated the group's liking when his self-esteem was low than when it was high.

It should be noted that the clinicians and Dittes consider self-esteem to be an invariant—they assume that the individual's level of self-esteem remains quite constant over time. They do not consider the possibility that an individual might have unusual confidence—or an unusual lack of confidence—in himself, and the effect that momentary self-esteem might have on his liking for others who accepted or rejected him. We might ask how *changes* in a person's self-esteem might affect his receptivity to accepting or rejecting individuals. The theoretical and experimental literature relevant to this question at first seems quite consistent with Dittes' proposal but quite contradictory to the clinicians' observations.

## Self-esteem and Romantic Liking

Walster (1965) proposed that an individual would like an affectionate other more when his own self-esteem had been recently *lowered* than when it was momentarily *raised*. This prediction agrees with that of Dittes (1959).

Walster gave two reasons for this prediction: First, a person with high self-esteem is likely to feel that since he has much to offer another, he, in turn, deserves a more attractive, more personable friend than would a person with lower self-regard and with less to offer another. Goffman makes a proposal consistent with this notion when he comments: "A proposal of marriage in our society tends to be a way in which a man sums up his social attributes and suggests to a woman that hers are not so much better as to preclude a merger or partnership in these matters" (1952, p. 456). In other words, Goffman is suggesting that the more highly a man evaluates himself and his own social attributes, the more perfection he'll feel a woman should possess in order to deserve him. If the above proposition is true, a given woman should appear more acceptable and desirable, and should be better liked by a man, when his self-esteem (and requirements) are low than when his self-esteem (and requirements) are high.

Second, a lowering of one's self-regard produces an increased need for the affection and regard of others. Thus, an affectionate person should be more attractive to an individual when his self-confidence has been shattered than when it is at its highest.

There are few other theorists who have advanced a proposal of this type. Reik (1944) argues that it is when one feels dissatisfied with oneself that he is especially susceptible to falling in love; as evidence he cites the observation that falling in love on the rebound, after one has suffered a severe blow to his ego, is common.

In an attempt to resolve the problem that some clinicians predict and demonstrate a positive relationship between self-esteem and liking for others, while other experimenters propose and demonstrate a negative relationship, Walster performed an experiment. She tested the following two relationships: (1) the effect of *changes* in self-esteem on one's liking for an affectionate other; and (2) the relationship between measured ("stable") self-esteem and liking for various others.

In order to assess the effect of changes in self-esteem on one's receptivity to romantic liking, the following procedure was utilized:

a.  A female subject was introduced to a male confederate who made it clear that he was romantically interested in her.

b.  The self-esteem of some girls was raised by giving them authoritative positive information about themselves; the self-esteem of other girls was lowered by giving them authoritative negative information about themselves.

c.  The girls were asked to rate the male confederate under conditions which would encourage them to give honest, frank replies.

Specifically, college women were hired to participate in a research project on personality processes. As part of this project, they were asked to complete the *California Personality Inventory* (CPI), during an initial session.

A short time before the subsequent testing session, the girl met a fellow, ostensibly by accident, who indicated that he was very interested in her. They met in the hall while both were presumably looking for the experimenter. The male began speculating with the girl in a friendly way about what the interviews were like and why the experimenter was late. Then he began telling her a little about himself. For approximately 15 minutes, he talked to her with the intention of conveying to her that he was personally interested in her and of asking her for a dinner and show date in San Francisco the following week. Soon after the date had been made, the experimenter arrived and directed the romantic partner to another experimental room.

Then the experiment proper began. The girl was given two personality tests, a word association test and the *Rorschach Ink Blot Test*. When testing was completed the girls were handed the "test results," but instead of their actual test scores, the girls were given a bogus personality report. The girls received either an extremely flattering or an extremely disparaging personality analysis. Which one they received was determined by chance. For those girls assigned to the Lowered-esteem condition, the analysis stressed the girl's "immaturity," her "weak personality, antisocial motives, lack of originality, and flexibility, and lack of capacity for successful leadership." For the girls assigned to the Raised-esteem condition, the report stressed the girl's great maturity and originality and her probable underestimation of her own attributes, and stated that she presented "one of the most favorable personality structures analyzed by the staff." The report also stressed "sensitivity to peers, personal integrity, and originality and freedom of outlook."

That people will accept false personality descriptions as accurate descriptions of themselves has been established previously (Bramel, 1962; Glass, 1964). That individuals would accept and trust a stranger's description of themselves rather than their own perceptions may seem strange, but it is a fact on which fortune-tellers rely.

The girl's liking for the male, after having her self-esteem momentarily raised or lowered, was assessed in a second experiment. As part of this experiment, girls were asked to give (anonymously) their honest reactions to five people: The male confederate who had asked for a date, the person she was most attracted to at the present time, the experimenter who had given her back the personality report, a specified teacher, and herself.

Women whose self-esteem had been temporarily lowered were more receptive to the confederate's affection than were women whose self-esteem had been temporarily raised. The average Low-esteem condition woman rated her liking for the partner in between "I like him extremely much" and "I like him fairly much." The average High-esteem condition woman indicated she felt fairly neutral about the partner.

It will be recalled that Walster (1965) also wished to investigate the relationship between stable self-esteem and one's liking for various others. We noted earlier that most clinicians argue that high stable self-esteem produces increased love of others, while the preceding study and Dittes (1959) found that lowered self-esteem produced more liking for a romantic partner or a work partner than did increased self-esteem. Is there any way that we can reconcile these contradictory results?

No definite answer to this question is available. However, there is some experimental evidence which provides a tentative reconciliation of these conflicting data. Walster (1965) proposed that in order to accurately predict the relationship that exists between self-esteem and liking for another, one must know whether the "other" is an accepting person or rejecting person.

As a basic point, Walster accepted Dittes' formulation that when an individual knows how the other feels about him, the more intensely that individual needs approval, the more strongly he will reciprocate the other's feelings: i.e., a low self-esteem person will like an accepting other better, and will dislike a rejecting other more than will a person higher in self-esteem.

What happens when the individual does not know whether the other accepts or rejects him? It is with just such situations that the clinicians have inevitably worked. Walster suggests that under ambiguous conditions, a high self-esteem person is likely to assume that the other likes him more than does a low self-esteem person. In a later chapter we will find that the more one thinks another likes him, the more he will reciprocate that liking. Thus, when subjects have no information as to whether or not the other accepts him, the clinicians' formulation that there is a positive relationship between self-esteem and liking seems most reasonable.

On the basis of this logic, Walster predicted that when the other makes clear his liking for the subject, there will be a negative relationship between self-esteem and liking. When the other makes clear his rejection of the subject, or when his feelings about the subject must be guessed, there will be a positive relationship between self-esteem and liking for the other. There is some evidence that the above proposal is correct. As part of the experiments discussed earlier, all subjects took the *California Personality Inventory.* Walster computed a measure of stable self-esteem for all her subjects by standardizing their scores on six CPI measures of Poise, Ascendency, and Self-assurance and averaging them together. The higher this average, the higher the girl's self-esteem was said to be. The girl rated both people who accepted her (the male confederate) and people who had given her no information as to their feelings toward her (a teacher and the experimenter). According to the above proposal, we expect a negative relationship between stable self-esteem and liking for the confederate. (Unfortunately, no ratings of those who rejected the girl were secured.) We should expect a positive relationship between the girl's self-esteem and her liking for the experimenter and the teacher. The correlations were as expected. Additional support for this hypothesis comes from a recent study by Jacobs, Walster and Berscheid (in preparation).

CHAPTER FOUR

# Rewards Others Provide: Propinquity

## PROXIMITY AS AN INTENSIFIER OF SENTIMENT

A frequently advanced and commonly accepted notion is that propinquity, or proximity, has a strong influence on one's friendship choices. Stated in its simplest form, the proposition is as follows: Other things being equal, the closer two individuals are located geographically, the more likely it is that they will be attracted to each other. Studies demonstrating the impact of proximity on friendship choices are so numerous that we will mention only a few.

Several investigators have collected data which indicate that students tend to develop stronger friendships with those students who share their classes, or their dormitory or apartment building, or who sit near them, than with those who are geographically located only slightly farther away (Maisonneuve, Palmade, and Fourment, 1952; Willerman and Swanson, 1952; Festinger, 1953; Byrne and Buehler, 1955; Byrne, 1961a). Clerks in a large department store and members of a bomber crew have been found to develop closer relations with those who happen to work next to them than with co-workers a few feet away (Gullahorn, 1952; Kipnis, 1957; Zander and Havelin, 1960).

One of the more interesting studies demonstrating the relationship between proximity and friendship choice was conducted by Festinger, Schachter, and Back (1950). These investigators examined the development of friendships in a new housing project for married students. The housing development studied consisted of small houses arranged in U-shaped courts, such that all except the end houses faced onto a grassy area. The two end houses in each court faced onto the street. Festinger (1951) arrived at the intriguing conclusion that to a great extent architects can determine the social life of the residents of their projects. According to Festinger:

> It is a fair summary to say that the two major factors affecting the friendships which developed were (1) sheer distance between houses and (2) the direction in which a house faced. Friendships developed more frequently between next-door neighbors, less frequently between people whose houses were separated by another house, and so on. As the distance between houses increased, the number of friendships fell off so rapidly that it was rare to find a friendship between persons who lived in houses that were separated by more than four or five other houses . . .
>
> There were instances in which the site plan of the project had more profound effects than merely to determine with whom one associated. Indeed, on occasion the arrangements of the houses severely limited the social life of their occupants . . . In order to have the street appear 'lived on,' ten of the houses near the street had been turned so that they faced the street rather than the court area as did the other houses. This apparently small change in the direction in which a house faced had a considerable effect on the lives of the people who, by accident, happened to occupy these end houses. They had less than half as many friends in the project as did those whose houses faced the court area. The consistency of this finding left no doubt that the turning of these houses toward the street had made involuntary social isolates out of the persons who lived in them . . .*

There were still other architectural features which were found by Festinger, Schachter, and Back to have important effects on the social life of the residents. Any architectural feature which brought an individual into proximity with other residents tended to increase his popularity. It was found, for example, that the positions of the stairways enabled the residents of the apartments near the entrances and exits of the stairways to make more friends than other residents. Similarily, the position of the mailboxes in each building improved the social life of the residents of the apartment near which they were located.

Many of the studies which have demonstrated the potency of proximity upon friendship formation have important social implications. It has been found, for example, that white persons who experience increased contact with Negroes become less prejudiced subsequent to that contact. This finding has been secured in such varied settings as in a meat packing plant (Palmore, 1955), a housing project (Deutsch and Collins, 1958), and in a university classroom (Mann, 1959). It is interesting that this finding, that integrated housing may produce increased racial harmony, has been the ammunition with which both integrationists and segregationists have

---

*Festinger, L. "Architecture and group membership," *J. Soc. Issues,* 1951, **1**, pp. 156-157.

defended their disparate points of view. Deutsch and Collins (1958), for example, concluded on the basis of these data that integrated housing should be encouraged since such integration helps eradicate racial prejudice. Segregationists, however, have concluded that since the evidence suggests that integration would lead to interracial friendships and "race mixing," segregation should be preserved at all costs.

Propinquity also has been found to be an important factor in mate selection. Several studies have demonstrated that there is an inverse relationship between the distance separating potential marriage partners and the number of marriages. One such study was conducted by Bossard (1932) who examined 5,000 marriage licenses in which one or both applicants were residents of Philadelphia. He found that 12 percent of the couples were already living at the same address at the time they applied for their license; one third of them lived within five or less blocks of each other. The percentage of marriages decreased steadily and markedly as the distance between the residences of the engaged couples increased. Corroboration of the importance of propinquity in mate selection comes from Abrams (1943), Kennedy (1943), and Katz and Hill (1958).

All of these data are compatible with the hypothesis that the less physical distance there is between two individuals, the more likely it is that they will become attracted to each other. But since these studies have focused upon friendship formation rather than "enemy formation," their findings do not disconfirm the equally plausible, but contrary, proposition that the less physical distance there is between two individuals, the more likely it is that they will dislike each other.

Evidence that close proximity to another may be likely to produce interpersonal hostility as well as interpersonal attraction comes primarily from police records, rather than from the social scientist's notebook. The Detroit Police Department's 1967 Annual Report, for example, indicates that in the majority of robberies the perpetrator was either related to, or acquainted with, the victim. It is somewhat surprising to find that thieves are much more likely to rob an intimate than a stranger. It would seem that if a thief had common sense, he would be careful to steal from someone who could not easily identify him. The evidence, however, indicates that individuals are most likely to victimize those in close proximity. Perhaps those ladies who fear the intrusion of "thieving maniacs" into their homes may be able to take some comfort from the fact that the intruder is likely to be a friend.

Aggravated assault, like thievery, appears also to be directed toward intimates. According to J. Edgar Hoover, "Most aggravated assaults occur within the family unit or among neighbors and acquaintances. The victim and offender relationship as well as the very nature of the attack make this crime similar to murders" (1966, p. 9). With respect to homicide, Hoover's statistics reveal that killings within the family make up almost a third of all murders. If one adds to this those which occur between "romantic lovers," the figure is even higher.

It seems logically clear, then, that distance *per se* does not have the strong consequences for positive attraction which the friendship-formation data suggest. While propinquity may be a necessary condition for attraction, it appears that it also may be a necessary condition for hatred.

## INCREASED PROBABILITY OF ACQUIRING INFORMATION

What underlies the often obtained relationship between proximity and sentiment? Obviously something is made possible, or more likely, with decreasing distance. It seems apparent that what is made possible is an increased probability of receiving information about another person and an increased probability of receiving rewards or punishments from the other. Sentiments such as liking or disliking, and especially the strong sentiments of love and hate, are not likely to be felt for people about whom we have minimal information and with whom we have had little experience. What proximity appears to allow, and what distance prevents, is an opportunity to obtain information and accumulate experience regarding the rewards or punishments we are likely to receive from the other person.

Can we conclude, then, that if we know the degree of proximity between two people, and do not have knowledge of the content of the information exchange such proximity has made possible, we cannot make a prediction concerning whether a positive sentiment or a negative sentiment will develop? There appear to be a number of factors which may make such a conclusion erroneous: It appears that there is a somewhat greater tendency for proximity to breed attraction than hostility.

Newcomb has advanced the hypothesis that proximity should produce positive rather than negative attraction. He argues that "... when persons interact, the reward-punishment ratio is more often such as to be reinforcing than extinguishing ..." (1956, p. 576). Thus, he reasons that the information which proximity permits is more likely to be favorable than unfavorable and that liking, therefore, will more often result from proximity than disliking. There is little direct evidence to support this proposition. Nevertheless, Newcomb's arguments do seem plausible. Since people are to a great extent dependent upon one another for the satisfaction of their needs, it seems probable that individuals generally take care to reward others as much as possible in interaction with them. In addition, social canons of courtesy often prohibit dealing out punishments to others even when one is so inclined.

### Heider's Balance Theory

There is yet another reason why close proximity with another may favor the development of positive rather than negative affect. The prediction that proximity will more often lead to liking than disliking can be derived from a number of the cognitive-consistency theories. It can perhaps be most easily derived from Heider's (1958) balance theory. The basic tenet of Heider's theory is that people strive to make their sentiment relationships harmonious with their perception of the unit relationships existent between objects.

What does Heider mean by the phrase *"sentiment relationships"*? A "sentiment" is simply a positive or negative attitude toward someone or something. What does Heider mean by the phrase *"unit relationships"*? Separate entities are said to have a unit relationship when they are perceived as belonging together. The members of a family, for example, are usually perceived of as a unit, as are a person and his clothing, and so on. In his discussion of the conditions which facilitate unit formation, Heider draws upon the principles of perceptual organization which were formulated by the Gestalt psychologists. The Gestaltists discovered that one relationship between objects which is especially likely to lead to unit formation is proximity: Objects which are close together spatially tend to be perceived as a unit. According to Heider's theory, then, if one perceives that a unit relationship with another exists (e.g., the other is in close promimity), this perception should induce a harmonious sentiment relationship (e.g., liking).

To test whether or not unit formation produced by the anticipation of interacting intimately with another would increase attraction, Darley and Berscheid (1967) led college women to expect that they were going to discuss their sexual standards and behavior with another girl, ostensibly participating in the same study. After the expectation of further interaction had been induced, each girl was given two folders. One folder was said to contain personality information about her partner, the girl with whom she would converse and exchange information. The other folder was said to contain information about another girl, who would also participate in the study but whom she would never meet. The personality information contained in both folders was designed to produce as ambiguous a picture as possible of the girl described.

Half of the subjects believed that the girl described in folder A was their "randomly selected" discussion partner; the other half believed that the girl described in folder B was their partner. Subjects were instructed to read through both folders, form a general impression of both girls, and then rate each of them along a number of dimensions, including liking.

The results of this study clearly indicated that the subjects expressed more liking for the girl who had been designated as their discussion partner than they did for the girl who was not.

This study suggests, then, that the factor of proximity, uncontaminated by the specific information which proximity often permits to be exchanged, may produce a feeling of unit formation between two people. This feeling of being in a unit relationship with another may then induce feelings of liking for that other. Knowledge that one will be in close proximity with another may result, then, in an individual's going *into* an interaction situation with increased liking for the other person prior to the actual interaction and prior to actual knowledge of possible rewards which may be obtained in the interaction.

It is interesting that the liking produced by the anticipation of being in close proximity with another may lead a person to voluntarily choose to associate with the other person, even though the original interaction which was anticipated has been cancelled. Berscheid, Boye, and Darley (1968) found that even when a subject anticipated interacting with an objectively undesirable person, the attraction induced by the anticipation of close interaction caused subjects to choose voluntarily to interact with that negative person more readily than did people who had not previously anticipated association with him.

In conclusion, then, actual proximity is probably correlated with attraction (or repulsion) because proximity allows one to obtain an increased amount of information about the other person and to experience rewards or punishments from the other. There is some suggestive evidence that proximity in and of itself, apart from any information it may provide about another and apart from any rewards or punishments which the other may administer, may facilitate attraction as a by-product of the individual's desire for cognitive consistency.

# CHAPTER FIVE

# Rewards Others Provide: The Reciprocity-of-Liking Rule

A naive observer from another culture would have little trouble discovering one reward which people in our society spend a tremendous amount of time, money, and effort to obtain. Just a brief glance at a few television commercials would reveal that the desire for the esteem of others must be a very strong and pervasive motivation, for it is often exploited by those who have something to sell. From girdles to car batteries, mouthwashes to cake mixes, the standard marketing technique is to convince the prospective buyer that the product will help him win admiration and affection—or, at the very least, allow him to avoid offending others and reaping their scorn. Countless everyday observations provide a great deal of evidence that we value highly the esteem of others and will work hard to obtain this reward. If esteem is indeed a reward, and if it is true that we tend to like those who reward us, it follows that we should like people who like us.

The proposition that esteem will be reciprocated can be derived from several psychological theories. Theorists who take the reinforcement point of view reason that the most general determinants of interpersonal esteem are reciprocal rewards and punishments. Some of these theorists (e.g., Homans, 1961) have specifically noted that one type of reward to which people are extremely responsive is social approval or esteem. Like money, social approval is viewed as a generalized, "transituational" reinforcer because it has the power to reinforce a wide variety of human activities. For example, many experimenters have demonstrated that if one merely nods his head and murmurs approval each time his discussion partner utters a plural noun, he can dramatically increase the frequency with which the recipient of that reward will pepper his discourse with plural nouns (e.g., Greenspoon, 1955; Dulany, 1961). Stronger demonstrations of approval, such as the roar of the crowd or another's love for oneself, frequently influence lifetimes of activity.

Social approval, again like money, is valuable because its possession makes one reasonably confident that a number of his needs will be satisfied; a lack of social approval often indicates that many of one's needs—those which require the good will and cooperation of others for satisfaction—will be frustrated.

In addition to the reinforcement theorists, cognitive-consistency theorists also make the reciprocal-liking prediction. Heider's balance theory (1958), for example, predicts that if Person A likes X (himself) and Person B likes X (Person A), a cognitively balanced state in which Person A likes Person B will be induced. Many correlational data, obtained from a wide variety of psychological studies, have been cited in support of the reciprocal-liking proposition (e.g., Newcomb, 1961). These data provide evidence that individuals tend to believe that the people they like reciprocate their liking. If it is true that we like people who like us, we would expect to find such a correlation. Taken alone, however, these data do not provide conclusive evidence for reciprocity of liking. Either one of two processes, or both, could be responsible for the observed correlation between the extent to which we feel another likes us and the extent to which we like him.

1.  A person may come to like another and *then,* as a consequence of his liking, come to perceive that the other person likes him. In such a case, the liking for the other is not induced by the other person's providing the reward of esteem, but rather by some other determinant of interpersonal attraction.

2.  One may become attracted to another as a consequence of his discovery that the other person likes him. Such a process would support the notion that esteem constitutes a reward, and we are attracted to people who give such a reward.

An experiment conducted by Backman and Secord (1959) was designed to investigate whether or not the latter process does indeed operate. To test the hypothesis that one will come to like those he discovers like him, the experimenters formed groups of strangers. Before the first meetings of the groups, they informed each subject that personality test analyses had revealed that certain designated others in his group would probably like him very much.

Each group then met for informal discussion. After group members had interacted, the experimenters informed the subjects that the group later might be broken into two-person teams. Subjects were asked to indicate from a list of the other group members their first, second, and third choices for persons they most desired as team partners. Each group met six times and sociometric data were collected at the first, third, and sixth sessions.

The results of Backman and Secord's experiment revealed that at the close of the first session, the subjects chose designated likers as desired team partners more often than they chose other members of the group. The data obtained from the first session, then, support the notion of reciprocal liking.

After additional sessions of group interaction, however, the data revealed that the designated likers were no longer chosen in preference to other group members. The reciprocity effect dissipated in the third and sixth sessions. Actual contact between group members apparently gave the subjects realistic information as to how much the other group members liked them, and thus decreased the importance of the information supplied by the experimenters as to who would probably like them.

Backman and Secord's experiment, then, suggests that if a person perceives another as liking him, he tends to be attracted to that other. What about the reverse process? If one is very attracted to another person, is he likely to overestimate the extent to which the other person finds him attractive? There are findings which suggest that this process also operates (e.g., Tagiuri, 1958).

We might suspect, however, that, here too, the tendency to assume that those we like also like us cannot withstand an abundance of evidence to the contrary, which may accumulate over repeated interactions. For example, no matter how much a person might wish to convince himself that the woman he loves reciprocates his affection, such a distortion becomes more and more difficult to maintain as the number of times she refuses to date him grows.

Although the tendency to like people who like us is sufficiently commonplace that the reciprocity-of-liking rule has been cited as a necessary and "non-empirical" principle of human behavior (Ossorio and Davis, 1966), life and literature appear to abound with exceptions. We will deal with the possible determinants of some of these exceptions next.

## THE INCONGRUENCY EXCEPTION

Most popular advice to those who would win the affection of others assumes that the reciprocity-of-liking rule will always hold true. For example, Dale Carnegie's injunction to those who would win friends and influence people—to be "hearty" in one's approbation and "lavish" in one's praise (1937, p. 51)—is based on this assumption. Though Carnegie's formula captured widespread interest in this country, it was pre-dated by several years in the writings of the philosopher Hecato (2nd century B.C.): "I will show you a love potion without drug or herb or any witch's spell; if you wish to be loved, love."

Despite the frequency with which advice to the contrary has been proffered, daily experience often demonstrates that the esteem of others is not always to be won through a demonstration of our own affection and admiration; indeed, if it were, the phenomenon of unrequited love would be unknown and many romantic novels never would have been written.

There are many possible reasons why esteem is not always followed by esteem. One especially interesting determinant of some of these instances can be derived from the cognitive-consistency theories. The reader will recall that many of the cognitive-consistency theories predict that if a Person A likes X (any object or person including Person A himself), and if Person B also likes X, then a balanced and psychologically comfortable state in which Person A likes Person B should be induced.

Ordinarily people do like themselves. If X happens to be Person A himself, and if Person B likes X, then Person A should like Person B in return. It infrequently may happen, however, that Person A may possess very low self-esteem and may *not* like X (himself). If Person B is perceived to like Person A very much, in spite of the fact that A views himself as dislikable, B's liking for A should produce an imbalanced, psychologically uncomfortable state for Person A. Under such conditions, Person B's liking for A, rather than causing A to reciprocate B's liking, should produce balance resolution in the form of Person A disliking Person B.

According to cognitive-consistency theory, then, we should like those who like us only if we like ourselves; if we dislike ourselves, we should dislike those whose feelings about us are positive, and thus incongruent with our own. Although this prediction follows clearly from balance theory, it is not a prediction that seems intuitively obvious. It reminds us of Groucho Marx's reasoning: "I wouldn't be caught dead joining any club that would have me as a member."

To test the hypothesis that one will evaluate most favorably those people whose evaluations of oneself are congruent with one's own, Deutsch and Solomon (1959) created an experimental situation in which each subject was led to evaluate her performance on a group of tasks either favorably or unfavorably. At this point another member of the group sent her a note. In this note, her team-mate either evaluated her performance very favorably and indicated she was a very desirable team-mate, or evaluated her performance very unfavorably and indicated she was not a very desirable team-mate. It was predicted that if the subject had given a successful performance, she would more favorably evaluate a team-mate who gave a favorable evaluation of her performance than one who gave an unfavorable evaluation. Conversely, if the subject had given an unsuccessful performance, it was predicted that she would more favorably evaluate a team-mate who gave an unfavorable evaluation of her performance than one who gave a favorable evaluation.

The results of this experiment indicated that when subjects had given a successful performance the investigators' prediction was confirmed: Subjects liked those who praised their performance and who wanted them as a team-mate. However, if subjects had given an unsuccessful performance, there appeared to be little difference in their reactions to favorable or to unfavorable evaluations: Evaluators who stated that the subject had given a successful performance, and who wanted the subject as a team-mate again, were liked just as much as those who did not, even though the friendly team-mate's evaluation was incongruent with the subject's own unfavorable evaluation of herself.

Deutsch and Solomon reasoned that their failure to obtain the predicted results in the unsuccessful-performance condition was due to a "positivity" effect, with the result that subjects tended to evaluate all positive notes more favorably than negative notes. Reinforcement theory would predict such a positivity effect: Esteem from others should be rewarding even if that esteem is cognitively incongruent with one's own poor self-image.

If such a positivity effect is posited, the results of the Deutsch and Solomon study do support the cognitive-consistency theory prediction, even though negative evaluators were not liked more than positive evaluators in the unsuccessful-performance condition. Since the favorable notes did not produce *more* esteem than unfavorable notes, we have suggestive evidence that the typical reinforcement effect of esteem may be attenuated when the esteem given is cognitively incongruent for the recipient.

This study provides little more than suggestive evidence on this proposition, however, because the data from the unsuccessful-performance condition may have been obtained for reasons other than the incongruity of the favorable evaluation. Subjects in the Deutsch and Solomon study who had performed very poorly were told by their evaluator, "I see that you have the lowest score for the team. I really think you did a fine job considering your situation. You are a valuable member of the team and I would very much like to have you on my team again." Subjects in this condition, who had performed extremely poorly, must have had some doubts about the evaluator's intelligence and/or her motives. Perhaps more important than the fact that the favorable evaluation was incongruent was that it revealed that the evaluator was most probably not very intelligent or was insincere and ingratiating. This might have been responsible for reducing the liking subjects might otherwise have felt for such a rewarding person as the favorable evaluator.

The above argument also holds true for those subjects who had made high scores and received incongruent evaluations. Subjects in this condition were told that although they had made a high score, they had done a poor job and the note-writer was very much opposed to having them on her team again. Although there is hardly a question of the evaluator's being ingratiating, the evaluation does seem a bit bizarre in terms of acknowledged performance.

Other studies have been addressed to the question of esteem incongruency, and while they are not completely invulnerable to the above criticism, they do provide us with additional information on the effect of incongruent esteem.

Dickoff (1961), for example, also studied the responses of a person to varying evaluations made by others. In this experiment, each subject presented a sample of her behavior to an interviewer stationed behind a one-way mirror. This behavior sample was solicited by the interviewer through use of questions designed to reveal, in a short time, the subject's personal history, her manner, and her values. During the interview, the interviewer allegedly recorded her impressions of the subject.

Following the interview, the interviewer and the subject were brought together and the subject was given the task of guessing the impression which she had made upon the observer. The subject did this by attempting to guess, in a series of 96 trials, which of three different attributes had been chosen by the interviewer to apply to the subject. In each trial the three attributes consisted of a positive personal trait, a neutral trait, and a negative personal trait.

Depending upon the treatment to which the subject was assigned, the interviewer either:

1.   responded with a uniformly positive evaluation (or, in other words, the most positive attribute was always the correct choice for the subject);

2.   made responses identical to those made by the subject herself in an earlier group-testing session; or

3.   systematically avoided all positive attributes in favor of uniformly choosing the neutral one on each item.

Thus, the experimental situation was one in which some subjects (the Positive-condition subjects) received an evaluation which was extremely and uniformly positive, some subjects (the Self-concept condition subjects) discovered that the interviewer's impression of them was quite congruent with their own self-concept, and some subjects (the Negative-condition subjects) learned that the interviewer had a rather neutral, evasive and, by implication, perhaps even a negative, impression of them.

Cross-cutting these variations was a variation in the instructions given to the subject before she attempted to guess what impression she had made upon the observer.

1.   Some subjects operated under "Accuracy" instructions and were told that the specific purpose of the experiment was to discover "how accurately people form impressions of others".

2.   The remainder of the subjects were given "Ulterior motive" instructions. Like subjects in the Accuracy condition, these subjects were told that the purpose of the experiment was to determine how people form impressions of others. However, no mention was made to these Ulterior-

motive subjects of the importance of accuracy. Instead, it was mentioned to these subjects that the interviewer wanted them to participate in an experiment of her own following the present session. The intent of the Ulterior-motive instructions was to make the interviewer appear dependent upon the subject's good will and to suggest that an ulterior motive might govern the interviewer's subsequent personality judgments of the subjects.

The major dependent variable in this experiment was, of course, the subject's impression of the observer. Like Deutsch and Solomon, Dickoff found a "positivity" effect. The results revealed a positive relationship between the favorability of the evaluation the subject received and the degree of attraction for the interviewer. It was especially clear that subjects disliked interviewers from whom they had received a relatively negative evaluation.

The results also showed that the extent to which the observer was dependent upon the subject's willingness to participate in a subsequent experiment had an effect upon attraction. A completely positive evaluation by the interviewer was much more successful in producing esteem when there was no ulterior motive possible. Evidently the positive evaluation was taken with a grain of salt when the subject knew the interviewer wanted something from her. As we might expect, difference in interviewer motive produced no significant differences in attraction for the interviewer in either the self-concept or the neutral condition.

Dickoff's experiment produced another interesting result: The level of a subject's attraction for the interviewer was almost entirely a function of the favorability of the interviewer's evaluation and bore no relation to the subject's self-esteem (which was measured when she arrived at the experiment). Heider's balance theory would have led us to predict that subjects high in self-esteem should have responded more positively to the highly favorable evaluations than subjects low in self-esteem, since the highly favorable evaluations should have been more congruent with the self-image of the high self-esteem subjects.

It is also interesting that in Dickoff's experiment, the self-concept condition and the positive condition produced, over-all, approximately the same amount of attraction. If we can assume that the self-concept evaluations were less favorable than were the positive evaluations, these results are similar to those obtained by Deutsch and Solomon and would seem to support the cognitive-consistency theory prediction that congruency of an evaluation, as well as positivity, is important in producing esteem.

Both the Deutsch and Solomon experiment and the Dickoff experiment, then, appear to support the notion that the extent to which another's esteem is congruent with one's own self-esteem may be a factor in determining whether or not liking will be reciprocated. The results of another study, conducted by Berscheid, Walster, and Walster (in preparation), also support this notion.

Each subject in this experiment received four evaluations of his personality, ostensibly made by four different people. Subjects were told that the evaluations by the four people had been made on the basis of the results of several personality tests the subjects had taken at the time they entered the university. They were told that their evaluators had been instructed to "guess" what the subject was like on the basis of this ambiguous information, write their impressions, and indicate how much they felt they would like the subject.

In actuality, the four evaluations were composed by the experimenters who had previously arranged for each subject to take part in another experiment in which each subject had filled out a self-concept questionnaire. On this questionnaire the subject had indicated which traits he felt were very characteristic of himself, as well as which traits he felt were very uncharacteristic. In addition, he had indicated how positive or negative he felt each trait to be. On the basis of each subject's self-concept questionnaire, the four evaluations were composed and varied in the following ways:

1.   The "Accurate-Positive" evaluation was composed of eight traits which the subject had previously marked as being very characteristic of himself, and which, in addition, the subject had indicated were very positive;

2.   The "Accurate-Negative" evaluation was composed of seven characteristic and positive traits (identical to those contained in the Accurate-Positive evaluation) and one trait which the subject had indicated was characteristic of himself but which he felt was a negative trait;

3.   The "Inaccurate-Positive" evaluation was made up of eight uncharacteristic and positive traits;

4.   The "Inaccurate-Negative" evaluation was composed of seven unncharacteristic positive traits (identical to those in the Inaccurate-Positive evaluation) and one negative uncharacteristic trait.

Each evaluation was concluded by a statement to the effect that the prospective team-mate thought he would like the subject very much. After reading the evaluations and the liking estimates, each subject rated each of the evaluators on a number of traits and, finally, indicated which of the four he wished to have as a team-mate. The results of this study revealed the ubiquitous "positivity" effect: Subjects were attracted more to those who gave positive evaluations than they were to those who gave negative ones.

The reader might be surprised that a positivity effect could be obtained when the Negative evaluation and the Positive evaluation conditions were so similar—when even the so-called "Negative" evaluation was actually overwhelmingly positive, and in addition, the evaluator had stated that he thought he would like the subject very much. In this connection, it is interesting to note that the results of a number of other experiments (e.g., Harvey, Kelley, and Shapiro, 1957) also indicate that people are extremely sensitive to the smallest degree of unfavorableness in statements of sentiment or evaluation from other people. One might speculate that this is due to the fact that in our society people are more often damned by faint praise than by out-and-out negative evaluation. Perhaps this is why people tend to become sensitive to a lack of enthusiasm in expressions of esteem. It has been observed that "Well, Well is a word of malice."

In addition to positivity, it was found that the extent to which an evaluation was accurate or inaccurate (congruent or incongruent with the subject's own image of himself) also strongly affected the amount of esteem given to the evaluator: Evaluators who gave congruent evaluations were liked much more than those who gave incongruent ones.

On the basis of these three studies, then, we can conclude that esteem does act as a positive reinforcer and produces reciprocal liking, but it is much more effective in producing liking when it is congruent with the subject's own evaluation of himself. Although cognitive-consistency theory would make such a prediction on the basis that the discomfort aroused by receiving incongruent esteem from another may be reduced by disliking that other, the studies cited do not show that this is necessarily the process mediating the effect. All the experimental results we have reported are liable to the interpretation that people who give incongruent evaluations are not very intelligent, and therefore, are less liked than those who maintain a more realistic view of the world.

## Do the Theories Conflict?

The reader with a long memory may conclude that he has discovered an inconsistency in the predictions made by psychologists, and in the data they report in support of their predictions. In this section we argued that although people in general do seem to prefer others who like them to those who dislike them, this effect should be especially pronounced when an individual has high self-esteem. If an individual has high self-esteem a person who expresses admiration for him is both rewarding and accurate. If an individual has low self-esteem, on the other hand, a person who expresses admiration is rewarding but inaccurate; the liking produced by the reward the other provides should be diminished by the knowledge that he is inaccurate.

The discerning reader will recall from Chapter 3, however, that both Dittes (1959) and Walster (1965) proposed that if an individual's self-esteem were temporarily lowered, he would be in greater need of esteem from others than he would be had his self-esteem been temporarily raised. In considering differences in need alone, they came to the conclusion that a person who expressed esteem for an individual would be better liked if that individual had low self-esteem (and was in great need of esteem) than if that individual possessed high self-esteem (and had little need for additional esteem). Conversely, the person who was rejecting was assumed to be more frustrating, and therefore less liked by the low self-esteem person than by the high self-esteem person.

Though at face value these two theories seem to counter each other when we try to predict how much a low or high self-esteem individual will like an accepting or rejecting person, reconciliation of the seemingly divergent results seems possible. A person can like another for many reasons. A person can claim to like another for very specific traits, about which the other already knows exactly how to accurately evaluate himself. ("I like you because you performed the task well—or badly"). Or he may claim to like another for unspecified reasons, or for traits unrelated to those on which the other has classified himself as good or bad. ("I like you for heaven knows what reasons, but certainly not for reasons that have anything to do with your task performance.") There is a crucial difference between the experiments designed to test the effect of accuracy on liking (which were reported in this chapter) and those experiments designed to test the effect of need on liking (which were reported in Chapter 3).

In those experiments which were designed to test the hypothesis that perceived accuracy or inaccuracy would have a crucial effect on how much an accepting or rejecting person was liked, B's esteem for the subject was always said to be based on the very traits on which A believed himself to be exceptional or inferior. As a result, B's esteem for A could easily be classified as accurate or inaccurate.

In the experiments designed to see what effect need for self-esteem would have on one's receptivity to affection, great care was taken to ensure that the proffered affection could not be classified as either an accurate or inaccurate reflection of the subject's traits. In Walster's study, for example, the girls' self-esteem was manipulated by telling them that they possessed varying degrees of maturity, personality strength, originality and flexibility, anti- or pro-social natures and various capacities for successful leadership. When the confederate expressed liking for the girl, it is unlikely that she perceived that his desire to date her had anything to do with her maturity or leadership potential. It seems far more probable that she assumed the confederate liked her because of her physical attractiveness, her conversational ability, or because they shared interests and experiences. Probably in all conditions, subjects assumed that the confederate's liking for her was based on an accurate perception of her qualities.

On the basis of the distinction we have drawn, we may conclude that:

1.  If another likes us for traits unrelated to those traits for which we admire or despise ourselves, the lower our general self-esteem the more we will appreciate affection and the more we will resent rejection.

2.  If another likes us for the very traits for which we admire or despise ourselves, the more accurate the other is the more we will like him in return.

## THE INGRATIATION EXCEPTION

In addition to the possibility that esteem received from another may be incongruent with the recipient's own self-image, there are a number of other factors which may operate to prevent a person from reciprocating the liking shown by another. One such factor concerns the fact that a person is usually quite aware that liking may be proffered to him for several different reasons. As a result, the recipient of esteem often makes a judgment as to the other's motivation by indicating that he holds him in high regard. The nature of this judgment may very well affect the extent to which esteem is reciprocated.

One judgment category into which expressions of esteem may be placed is "ingratiation." Ingratiation is the act of giving esteem to another with the view in mind of obtaining rewards or benefits from the recipient. There is evidence that when an expression of esteem is labeled—correctly or not—by the recipient as ingratiation, the probability that esteem will be given in return is reduced drastically.

In the Dickoff study previously described, for example, the interviewer who gave positive evaluations in the Non-Ulterior-Motive (Accuracy) condition was seen by subjects as "very likable and desirable as a friend." When the possibility of an ulterior motive was present, however, subjects saw the interviewer who gave positive evaluations as "defensive, fearful of creating a scene, not too bright, and generally insecure."

Subjects in the Dickoff experiment had concrete information that the giver of esteem wanted to use them later for her own experiment and, therefore, the possibility of an ulterior motive underlying her evaluations was readily apparent. In real life, of course, it is often difficult to be certain whether esteem is given with an ulterior motive or not. There are, however, various ways by which we make intelligent guesses.

One way in which we attempt to determine whether or not an ulterior motive may have prompted the expression of esteem is to evaluate the *grounds* upon which the esteem sentiment ostensibly was made. Such an evaluation of grounds is made possible by the fact that people seldom simply say "I like you." Rather, the "I like you" phrase usually is followed by "because . . . ," or, if not, some event noticeable to the esteem recipient obviously has prompted the remark. In cases in which the expression of esteem is not followed by a verbal reason for it, or no particular event or bit of behavior has seemed to have caused the remark, it is customary for the recipient to ask "Why do you say that?"

An expression of esteem, then, is a gift horse whose mouth is usually examined quite carefully. If the grounds upon which the esteem is given seem to be patently false, we are often led to suspect that esteem, since it is proffered for the *wrong* reason, has been expressed to obtain something for the ingratiator.

The tendency for the recipient of esteem to evaluate the grounds upon which the expression of esteem has been made has been well recognized by advisers in the art of winning love. Finck, for example, writing in 1891, advises his readers and would-be lovers that "Sincerity in compliments is essential, else all is lost. It is useless to try to convince a woman with an ugly mouth or nose that these features are not ugly. She knows they are ugly, as well as Rubinstein knows when he strikes a wrong note" (1891, p. 245).

We have already presented evidence that the more accurate (congruent with the recipient's own image) a positive evaluation is, the more likely it is that esteem will follow. The preceding discussion suggests that accurate evaluations may be effective not only because people wish to maintain cognitive consistency between their own evaluations and the evaluations of others, or because accuracy of evaluation implies higher intelligence and sensitivity than inaccuracy, but perhaps because accurate evaluations imply legitimate grounds for the expression of esteem and tend to rule out ingratiation motives.

There are, however, several obstacles to concluding that expressions of esteem should always be based on *totally* accurate evaluations in order to assure that esteem will be reciprocated. There is evidence that the recipient of a favorable evaluation often has a tendency to believe that the basis upon which the evaluation was made is indeed an accurate picture of himself, whether in reality it is or not. Such a tendency was observed in a study conducted by Jones, Gergen, and Davis (1962). In this experiment, subjects were asked to tell about themselves in an interview and were given either:

1. an "accuracy set," in which they were requested to give an honest and accurate picture of themselves and not to mislead the interviewer, or

2. an "ingratiation set," in which they were instructed to create the most favorable picture they could of themselves in the interview. Ingratiation subjects were instructed that the picture they presented did not necessarily have to be an honest one, since their task was to impress the interviewer.

Following the interview, subjects were given either positive feedback (i.e., the interviewer gave his impressions of them along with a statement of his positive esteem), or negative feedback (i.e., the interviewer's impressions were accompanied by a statement of negative sentiment). The results of this study showed a highly significant tendency for subjects who received positive feedback to report that their self-representations had been more *accurate* than did those who received negative feedback.

There is a second obstacle to concluding that the grounds upon which esteem is given must be totally accurate. A number of theorists on this topic are in agreement that the evaluation grounds should not be *too* obviously true. Finck, for example, while stating that accuracy is essential, also states that "The most common mistake of lovers is to compliment a woman on her most conspicuous points of beauty. This has very much the same effect on her as telling Rubinstein he is a wonderful pianist. He knows that better than you do, and has been told it so many times that he is sick and tired of hearing it again." Finck then goes on to quote Lord Chesterfield's dictum, " 'Very ugly or very beautiful women . . . should be flattered on their understanding, and mediocre ones on their beauty' " (1891, p. 245).

The above seems to imply that while evaluation grounds should not be patently false, they also should not be patently true. Jones (1964) discusses this interesting point along with somewhat related evidence and suggests that compliments are especially effective if the recipient is *uncertain* about the degree to which he possesses the attribute being complimented. There is, unfortunately, no direct evidence to support this hypothesis.

There are factors other than inaccurate grounds for esteem which may cause an expression of esteem to be seen as ingratiating and, thus, reduce the likelihood that the esteem will be reciprocated. When the giver of esteem, for example, is in no way dependent on the recipient for satisfaction of his needs (and thus an ulterior motive seems improbable) the expression of esteem appears to be much more likely to elicit esteem in return (e.g., Jones, Jones, and Gergen, 1963; Jones and Jones, 1964). For a discussion of this and other factors involved in ingratiation, the interested reader should see Jones (1964).

## THE SEQUENCE EXCEPTION

Another factor which appears to determine whether or not esteem will produce esteem in return is the patterning of one's expressions of esteem. It will be recalled that reinforcement theory predicts that since esteem is a reward, we will like those who provide us this reward. It follows from this position that the more esteem a person gives us, the more we should like him. We have already cited some evidence which appears to support this proposition. In the Dickoff study, for example, we noted that the investigators found that liking was very highly correlated with the positivity of the series of evaluations. Does this imply, then, that when esteem is consistently and frequently given, it is most likely to be reciprocated?

According to some theorists the answer to this question is "no." The relationship between being liked and liking others is somewhat more complex. Specifically, it is contended that the feeling of "gain" or "loss" produced by expressions of esteem is extremely important in determining whether or not esteem will be given in return: ". . . a gain in esteem is a more potent reward than invariant esteem, and similarly, a loss of esteem is a more potent 'punishment' than invariant negative esteem" (Aronson and Linder, 1965, p. 156).

On the basis of this reasoning, Aronson and Linder predicted that a person would be liked more if his behavior toward another was initially negative, but gradually became more positive, than if his behavior had been uniformly positive. Similarly, they predicted that if a person's initial evaluations were quite positive, but then gradually became more and more negative, that person would be disliked more than one who gave uniformly negative evaluations.

In the Aronson and Linder experiment each subject interacted with a confederate (who appeared to be another naive subject) over a series of seven meetings. Without intending to, the subject overheard an interview between the experimenter and the confederate (presumably a fellow student) and heard herself evaluated by the confederate after each of the meetings. The confederate's evaluations followed one of four patterns: (1) Negative-Positive, (2) Positive-Positive, (3) Negative-Negative, and (4) Positive-Negative.

In the Negative-Positive condition, the confederate expressed a negative impression of the subject during the first three interviews with the experimenter. Specifically, she described her as being a dull conversationalist, a rather ordinary person, not very intelligent, as probably not having many friends, etc. During the fourth session the confederate began to change her opinion of the subject. Her attitude became more favorable with each successive meeting until, in the seventh interview, it was entirely positive.

In the Positive-Positive condition, the confederate's stated opinions were invariably positive. During the seventh interview her statements were precisely the same as those stated in the seventh interview of the Negative-Positive condition.

In the Negative-Negative condition, the confederate invariably expressed negative feelings about the subject throughout the seven interviews.

The Positive-Negative condition was the mirror image of the Negative-Positive condition. The confederate began by stating that the subject seemed interesting, intelligent, and likeable, but by the seventh session she described the subject as being dull, ordinary, etc.

In the Positive-Positive condition the confederate made 28 favorable statements about the subject and no unfavorable statements. In the Negative-Negative condition the confederate made 24 unfavorable statements about the subject and no favorable ones. In both the Negative-Positive and Positive-Negative conditions the confederate made 14 favorable and 8 unfavorable statements about the subject.

At the close of the experiment, the subject was asked how much she liked the confederate. As Table 5.1 indicates, the results of this study confirmed the authors' hypothesis. Subjects liked the confederate better when her evaluations began by being negative, but gradually became positive, than when her evaluations had been uniformly positive. The confederate was liked less when her evaluations moved from positive to negative, than when they had been uniformly negative. The results of this experiment have been corroborated by the results of another conducted by Sigall and Aronson (1967).

*TABLE 5.1*

*Means and Standard Deviations for Liking
of the confederate*

| Experimental condition | Mean | SD | t-values | |
|---|---|---|---|---|
| 1. Negative-Positive | +7.67 | 1.51 | 1 vs. 2 | 2.71[+] |
| 2. Positive-Positive | +6.42 | 1.42 | 2 vs. 3 | 7.12[‡] |
| 3. Negative-Negative | +2.52 | 3.16 | 3 vs. 4 | 1.42[*] |
| 4. Positive-Negative | +0.87 | 3.32 | | |

[*]$p < .15$.
[+]$p < .02$.
[‡]$p < .001$ (all $p$ levels are two-tailed).

What could be responsible for such an effect? Several explanations are possible. Aronson and Linder suggest that the confederate who starts out with a negative evaluation creates in the subject anxiety, hurt, anger, self-doubt, etc. These feelings produce a "negative drive state." When the evaluator's behavior becomes more positive, her behavior is not only rewarding in and of itself, but it also is rewarding because it reduces the existing negative drive state which was previously aroused. The total reward value of the confederate's positive behavior is therefore greater in the Negative-Positive condition than in the Positive-Positive condition. The authors use similar reasoning to explain the "loss" portion of their results: When negative behavior follows positive behavior, it is not only punishing in its own right, but it also eradicates the positive effect associated with the rewarding nature of the evaluator's earlier behavior. It is reasoned that subjects disliked the positive-negative evaluator more than the entirely negative evaluator precisely because, in the first case, the evaluator had previously been rewarding.

The results of this experiment, then, suggest that a gain in esteem is a more potent reward than the absolute level of esteem itself. "After 10 years of marriage, if a doting husband compliments his wife on her appearance, it may mean very little to her. She already knows that her husband thinks she is attractive. A sincere compliment from a relative stranger may be much more effective, however, since it constitutes a gain in esteem. On the other hand, if the doting husband (who used to think his wife was attractive) were to tell his wife that he had decided that she was quite ugly, this would cause a great deal of pain since it represents a distinct loss of esteem" (Aronson and Linder, 1965, p. 60). One interesting implication of the gain-loss notion is that "you always hurt the one you love"; once we have grown certain of receiving rewards from another person (e.g., a husband or a close friend), that person may become less potent as a source of reward than a stranger since rewards received do not constitute gains. On the other hand, Aronson and Linder point out that "... the constant friend and rewarder has great potential as a punisher. The closer the friend, the greater the past history of invariant esteem and reward, the more devastating is its withdrawal. Such withdrawal, by definition, constitutes a loss of esteem" (1965, p. 169).

## DEPRIVATION AND SATIATION

The gain-loss notion of esteem leads us to consideration of another factor which often appears to affect the probability that esteem will be reciprocated. If a gain in esteem adds to the degree to which any given expression of esteem is perceived as rewarding, we might hypothesize that if a person were subjected to a period of deprivation of social approval he might, following this period of deprivation, respond more strongly, with more positive affect, to an expression of esteem from another person than if he had not experienced such deprivation. Similarly, we might hypothesize that if the recipient of esteem had received an unusually great amount of social approval and approbation in the immediate past, he might be less responsive to expressions of esteem than he would normally be.

These and similar hypotheses have been tested by a number of investigators (e.g., Gewirtz and Baer, 1958a, 1958b; Stevenson and Odom, 1962; Dorwart, Ezerman, Lewis, and Rosenhan, 1965). Gewirtz and Baer (1958a; 1958b), for example, demonstrated that the effectiveness of the reinforcement of social approval for modifying task performance is increased by a brief period of social isolation preceding performance of the task. They interpreted their results as indicating that the effectiveness of a social reinforcer is increased by its own deprivation.

Stevenson and Odom (1962) subsequently pointed out that a second interpretation of the Gewirtz and Baer experiment is possible. In the Gewitz and Baer experiment, the children who served as subjects were left with no toys or materials with which to amuse themselves during the period of deprivation preceding task performance and social reinforcement. Thus, isolation resulted, not only in deprivation of social stimuli, but of other types of stimuli as well. Stevenson and Odom reasoned that had the children not been subjected to general stimulus deprivation, but merely to deprivation of *social* stimuli, it is possible that the effectiveness of social reinforcers following such deprivation would not have increased.

To investigate this possibility, Stevenson and Odom studied the effect of social reinforcement upon children's performance in a simple operant task under three conditions:

1.   A Control condition in which children were not isolated before performance of the task.

2.   A "Toy" condition in which each child was deprived of *social* stimuli, but was left alone in a room filled with unusual and interesting toys with

which he could play freely for a 15 minute period.

3.   An "Isolation" condition in which each child was left alone in a room with no toys for 15 minutes preceding performance of the task.

The dependent variable in this experiment was, of course, the effectiveness of the experimenter's social and verbal reinforcement of the subject's performance on a marble-dropping task.

The results of the Stevenson and Odom experiment indicated a significant difference among conditions: The Isolation group showed the greatest increase in response rate after the first minute of the task and the control group the least increase. The performance of the Toy group did not differ significantly from that of the Isolation group.

The results were interpreted as tentatively supporting the hypothesis that increased effectiveness of social reinforcement following isolation is primarily dependent upon deprivation of social stimuli rather than upon general stimulus deprivation. Thus, this experimentation suggests that perhaps esteem is most likely to be reciprocated when the recipient has received a less than usual amount of attention and esteem from others in the immediate past; esteem is least likely to be reciprocated when the specific expression of esteem has been preceded by an exceptionally large amount of attention and esteem from others.

If it is true that it is a gain in esteem to which the recipient responds, rather than to the absolute level of esteem itself, we might hypothesize, as Aronson and Linder have suggested, that expressions of esteem from strangers generally receive more positive response than expressions of esteem from parents or people from whom one has become accustomed to receiving such rewards. A number of experiments have addressed this issue and have supported the notion that strangers are indeed generally more effective as agents of social reinforcement than are more familiar people (e.g., Shallenberger and Zigler, 1961; Stevenson and Knights, 1962; Stevenson, Keen and Knights, 1963; Harvey, 1962; Harvey, Kelley and Shapiro, 1957).

Such evidence, along with the gain-loss notion, leads us to the hypothesis that a person whose level of self-esteem has been temporarily lowered might be more responsive to an expression of esteem from another person than he ordinarily would be. Such an expression would constitute more of a gain in his recovering his good self-image than if his self-esteem had not been lowered temporarily. Similarly, a person whose self-esteem has been raised temporarily by some event might be less responsive than usual to an expression of esteem and less likely to reciprocate by giving esteem in return. Experimentation to test and support these hypotheses (e.g., Dittes, 1959 and Walster, 1965) was discussed in some detail in Chapter 3.

# CHAPTER SIX

# Rewards Others Provide: Similarity

The idea that people tend to like those similar to themselves is certainly not original with social psychologists. The tired adage, "Birds of a feather flock together," was old in Aristotle's time. Folk psychology, as expressed in such proverbs, is occasionally useful to the social scientist because it may sum up a wealth of human experience and wisdom. Frequently, however, folk psychology proves to be frustrating, and the "birds of a feather" notion is a case in point. As Newcomb (1956) has pointed out, this particular "law" of human behavior has limited usefulness because it is indiscriminate. People may be similar or different on any conceivable dimension upon which humans can be placed, and it seems quite unlikely that such similarities as length of big toe or social security number lead to attraction. In addition to being indiscriminate, folk psychology is often frustrating for another reason: One no sooner finds a maxim which appears to predict for a particular situation than one finds another which offers contradictory advice—in this case, "Opposites attract."

In this chapter we will explore some of the types of similarity or dissimilarity that facilitate interpersonal attraction.

## SIMILARITY OF ATTITUDES

A great deal of research effort has focused upon the relationship between attitudinal similarity and interpersonal attraction. One hypothesis which has received a great deal of attention is that people will like those who possess attitudes similar to their own. A second hypothesis is that people will *perceive* themselves as being more similar to those they like, and less similar to those they abhor, than they really are. Both of these hypotheses, that attraction leads to the perception of similarity, and the converse, that perception of similarity leads to attraction, can be derived from a number of cognitive-consistency theories. Perhaps, however, they can be most easily derived from Heider's balance theory (1958), which was discussed in Chapter 4.

It will be recalled that Heider proposed that people strive to make their sentiment relationships harmonious with their perception of the unit relationships existent between objects. According to Heider, separate entities which are *similar* tend to be perceived as belonging together (having a unit relationship). According to Heider's theory, then, positive unit formation (e.g., perceived similarity) should induce a harmonious sentiment relationship (e.g., liking). This process, of course, should also operate in reverse: Liking for another should lead to the perception that a harmonious unit relationship exists (e.g., that the liked other is similar to oneself).

### Evidence that Liking Causes the Perception of Similarity.

There is support for the proposition that individuals who like one another perceive themselves as being more similar than they really are. Investigators have measured both the amount of *perceived* similarity and the amount of *actual* similarity which exists between those who like one another. These findings indicate that individuals often overestimate the extent to which their friends share their attitudes. Both Byrne and Blaylock (1963) and Levinger and Breedlove (1966), for example, have found that the amount of attitudinal similarity which actually exists between husbands and wives is significantly less than the amount of similarity the spouses assume exists. While the higher magnitude of assumed similarity may be the result of needs for cognitive consistency, it may also be that husbands and wives tend to emphasize their similarities and to conceal or to avoid areas of disagreement in the interest of harmony.

The proposition that liking leads to perceived similarity receives its strongest support from studies in which feelings of attraction have been induced on bases other than attitudinal similarity and in which actual interaction between pairs has not occurred. One such study was conducted by Byrne and Wong (1962). Subjects who possessed varying degrees of prejudice against Negroes were asked to estimate how similar the attitudes of a Negro stranger and a white stranger were to their own. Prejudiced subjects assumed that they would agree with the Negro less often than they would agree with the white stranger. Unprejudiced subjects assumed that the Negro stranger and the white stranger were equally likely to share their attitudes. It appears, then, that the subject's liking (for Negroes) influenced his perception of how similar or dissimilar another's attitudes were likely to be to his own.

### Evidence that Attitudinal Similarity Produces Liking

A great deal of research has focused upon the second proposition which was derived from Heider's theory: That actual attitudinal similarity will produce interpersonal attraction. Newcomb (1961) examined development of friendship among a group of male students at the University of Michigan. All the men were strangers when they arrived at Michigan and at the dormitory which they had been assigned to share. As we might expect on the basis of studies mentioned in the previous section, Newcomb found that the more a man liked another resident, the more he tended to assume that the other would agree with him on important and relevant matters.

Newcomb also found support for the general hypothesis that given adequate opportunity for individuals to become familiar with each other's attitudes, attraction is indeed predictable from actual attitudinal agreement. Newcomb found that the correlation between a man's liking for another and the extent to which they actually agreed concerning the attractiveness of the other residents, increased with acquaintance. The positive relationship between attraction and agreement became statistically significant only in the final weeks of the study. Newcomb found a similar relationship between attraction and similarity on other attitudes and values: From a knowledge of how similar individuals were *before* moving into the dormitory, one could predict who would be attracted to whom on long acquaintance, but not who would be friends initially. It evidently took students a certain amount of time to discover which house members held attitudes similar to their own and which held dissimilar attitudes.

Other studies, of a more experimental nature, have also supported the proposition that attitude similarity is a determinant of interpersonal attraction. Many of these experiments have been conducted by Byrne and his associates, who have developed from their work a precise view of the effect of attitudinal similarity upon attraction.

Byrne and Nelson (1965), for example, compared the effect upon attraction of the *proportion* of similar attitudes expressed by a stranger with the effect of the *number* of similar attitudes expressed. To examine the relative effects of proportion and number of similar attitudes, each subject in their experiment was asked to read an attitude scale purportedly filled out by an anonymous stranger. Following completion of this task, each subject was requested to evaluate the stranger along a number of dimensions, including that of attraction. The attitude scales read by the subjects were composed by the experimenters in such a way that the number of similar attitudes expressed was varied parametrically. Cross-cutting variation on number of similar attitudes expressed was parametric variation of the proportion of similar attitudes expressed.

The results of this experiment indicated that attraction was significantly affected only by the proportion of similar attitudes expressed. The greater the proportion of similar, as opposed to dissimilar, attitudes, the greater the liking for the stranger who purportedly had filled out the attitude scale. In addition, the results suggested that the functional relationship between proportion of similar attitudes and attraction was linear.

Subsequent studies conducted by Byrne and his associates have corroborated the finding that interpersonal attraction is a positive linear function of the proportion of attitude statements attributed to an individual which are in agreement with the attitudes of the subject (e.g., Byrne and Clore, 1966; Byrne and Griffitt, in press). This effect seems to operate even with young children (Byrne and Griffitt, 1966).

At this point we might consider why it is that people find attitudinal similarity rewarding. Why should similarity lead to liking? We have previously mentioned one reason why attitudinal similarity may produce attraction: An individual's desire for cognitive consistency is served by liking those who hold attitudes similar to his own (assuming of course, that the individual likes himself). There are a number of other possible reasons why attitudinal similarity may be rewarding.

Festinger's theory of social comparison processes (1954), for example, also predicts a positive relationship between similarity and attraction and provides insight into the processes which may underlie the relationship. According to Festinger, people learn quite early in life that holding incorrect opinions and beliefs can be punishing, or even fatal, in many situations. Most people have, therefore, a drive to evaluate the correctness of their opinions and beliefs. A belief's "correctness" can be tested against two sources: physical reality or social reality. (Social reality is, of course, provided by the opinions and attitudes of others.) When we find that somebody else expresses the same attitudes and opinions we hold on an issue, we are given support for the notion that our own attitude is the correct one; the attitude is given social validation. Since it is presumably pleasant to feel that we have an objective and correct view of the world, such social validation should be rewarding. Or, as Byrne has stated, ". . . any time that another person offers us validation by indicating that his percepts and concepts are congruent with ours, it constitutes a rewarding interaction and, hence, one element in forming a positive relationship. Any time that another person indicates dissimilarity between our two notions, it constitutes a punishing interaction and thus one element in forming a negative relationship. Disagreement raises the unpleasant possibility that we are to some degree stupid, uninformed, immoral, or insane" (1961, p. 713).

Attitudinal similarity may produce attraction for still another reason. Attitudes often predict another's future behavior. If a person says that he thinks playing mumblety-peg is one of the most fascinating pastimes life has to offer, we may reasonably expect that he will engage in playing this game at every possible opportunity. Thus, if we ourselves relish mumblety-peg we may like another who expresses a positive attitude toward the game—not for reasons of cognitive consistency or for reasons of social validation, but simply because we anticipate many rewarding interactions, playing the game with the person who has expressed the positive attitude. An expression of a similar attitude towards some object, then, often implies that concrete rewards will follow in an interaction with that person; a dissimilarity in attitude often implies that one's needs will be frustrated.

There is still another reason why attitudinal similarity leads to liking. In Chapter 5 we found that people tend to like those who like them. It may be the case that when we learn another is similar to us, we assume that he is likely to like us, and thus we in turn like him.

Evidence that individuals tend to assume that similar others are likely to like them can be gleaned from an experiment by Walster and Walster (1963). These authors wondered why it is that individuals are found so consistently to seek out similar others and to avoid dissimilar others. That individuals should always prefer the company of similar others is *not* intuitively obvious. After all, associating with people very different from oneself has certain advantages—dissimilar others can provide new information and new insights into life, they may be unpredictable and thus exciting, etc. The authors reasoned that individuals might more often choose to associate with dissimilar others if one factor was not restraining them: Namely the fear that they will not be as well liked by dissimilar others as they are by similar others. When people are very different from oneself, their social standards are unclear; one is likely to be afraid that his behavior will be unacceptable if he is not quite sure how he is expected to behave, or what he is "supposed" to believe. For example, the gentlemanly Proust (1928) expressed fear that "boors and bounders," unaware of society's rule, would underrate *his* social value. It is probably more usual for one to be afraid of being rejected by those superior to himself.

The authors proposed that if students were confident that everyone they came in contact with would like them, they would be unusually anxious to associate with dissimilar strangers. On the other hand, they proposed that when it is especially important to be liked, or when one is unsure of his likability, he will be especially likely to "play it safe," and will be unusually anxious to associate with similar people.

These hypotheses were tested in the following way: College students were informed that they had been assigned to participate in one of several discussion groups set up to obtain information about why people dream. Students were told that they could participate in any one of five groups. Some groups consisted of people very similar to the subject (i.e., fellow students in introductory psychology). Other groups consisted of very dissimilar others (i.e., factory workers, psychologists, etc.).

Students were then led to have different expectations as to how much members of *all* groups would probably like them: (1) some subjects were assured that others would be predisposed to like them; (2) some were assured that others would be predisposed to dislike them; (3) some were instructed to choose a group in which others were likely to like them; (4) some (control subjects) were given no special instructions.

As predicted, it was found that if students were told it was important to talk with people who would like them, they more often chose to interact with similar than with dissimilar people. Apparently, they did assume that similar people were more likely to like them than were dissimilar people.

The authors' hypotheses were also supported. Those students who had been assured that everyone would find them likable, were much more willing to associate with dissimilar people than were subjects in the other conditions. In fact, they vastly preferred dissimilar groups to similar ones. Those students who were instructed that they probably would not be liked by any group members were more anxious to talk with similar people than were control subjects. It appears then that the more concerned one is about whether or not others will like him, the more anxious he will be to associate with similar others. Presumably, one has more hope of winning over similar strangers than dissimilar ones.

The finding that people who are psychologically secure are especially likely to associate with dissimilar others was corroborated by Goldstein and Rosenfeld (in press). Psychological security, in this research, was assessed by the Crowne-Marlowe Social Desirability Scale and Maslow's Security-Insecurity Inventory.

On the basis of the observation that people expect that similar others will like them, Aronson and Worchel (1966) have taken issue with Byrne's interpretation of his finding that interpersonal attraction is a positive function of attitude similarity. Byrne has chosen to interpret his data almost exclusively in terms of the consensual validation possibility: we like those who give us information that our attitudes are correct. Aronson and Worchel, however, have charged that this interpretation may be at least partially incorrect. They have reasoned that the similarity-liking relationship is due in part to an implicit assumption that people who hold attitudes similar to our own will like us. They have pointed out that in most of Byrne's experiments the only information the subject has about the other person is that many of his attitudes are similar to the subject's own. Aronson and Worchel have argued that if a similar or dissimilar other were to actually express either liking or disliking for the subject, the similarity or dissimilarity of the other's attitudes would have a negligible effect upon the subject's liking for the other; only the other's expression of liking or disliking would have an effect.

To test their hypothesis, Aronson and Worchel led students to believe that their partner in the experiment (who was in reality a confederate) had attitudes either very similar to or very unlike their own. In some cases the student was told explicitly that his partner liked him. The confederate was said to have stated that he was enjoying working with the subject, and that the subject seemed to be "a really profound and interesting person, well-informed." In other cases, the student learned that the other disliked him; the confederate stated that he had not enjoyed working with the subject in the experiment and, further, that the subject seemed to be a shallow and uninteresting person, not well informed.

Aronson and Worchel's results indicated a significant main effect due to liking. That is, whether or not the confederate stated in his evaluation that he liked the subject had an important effect on how much the subject liked the confederate. The results also indicated that attitudinal similarity had *no* effect upon liking. Whether or not the confederate expressed attitudes similar or dissimilar to the subject's appeared to have no significant influence upon the subject's subsequent liking for the confederate.

If Byrne's interpretation of the similarity-liking finding is correct, if it is true that consensual validation is rewarding even if the anticipated esteem from the other does not materialize, Aronson and Worchel should have found a similarity effect. Byrne and Griffitt (in press) reasoned that Aronson and Worchel's failure to find an effect of attitudinal similarity upon attraction was attributable to Aronson and Worchel's use of a restricted range of attitudinal similarity and dissimilarity. To investigate this possibility, Byrne and Griffitt replicated the Aronson and Worchel design and procedure with only one difference: They extended the range of attitudinal similarity-dissimilarity.

The results of their experiment indicated that both the like-dislike variable and the dissimilarity-similarity variable yielded highly significant effects upon interpersonal attraction. While the results of these experiments leave open the possibility that attitudinal similarity may produce liking because of anticipation of esteem from the other, it is clear that attitudinal similarity is rewarding even when such esteem is not forthcoming.

## Limitations to the Rule that Similarity Engenders Liking

While a positive relationship between attitudinal similarity and attraction has been found with great regularity, one can readily imagine that some limitations exist to the rule that attitudinal similarity engenders attraction.

One such limitation has been experimentally investigated by Byrne (1961). In this experiment Byrne was interested in examining whether a person who shared one's opinions on important issues would be better liked than one who had similar opinions on trivial matters. Byrne agreed with Newcomb (1961) that the *relevance* of the object of the attitude to the person holding the attitude will help determine how much perceived similarity affects liking. Byrne's prediction seems to be a reasonable one: We might reasonably expect an individual to develop more affection for a person who espouses the views one cherishes, than for a person who agrees on matters one considers relatively unimportant. You might expect to engender greater liking in segregationists by telling them you agree with their racial opinions than by telling them that you, too, agree that Edgar Guest was a great poet.

To test this hypothesis, Byrne asked his subjects to complete an attitude questionnaire and to indicate which issues mentioned in the questionnaire were most important to them and which were least important. Two weeks later, subjects were then given a questionnaire, ostensibly filled out by a person in another class. The responses on the questionnaires which subjects received were contrived in such a way that (a) one group of subjects received questionnaires expressing exactly the same attitudes the subjects themselves had expressed when they filled out their questionnaires; (b) a second group received questionnaires which expressed views opposite to their own; (c) another group received questionnaires which expressed similar opinions on issues subjects had indicated were most important, and dissimilar opinions on issues subjects had indicated were least important; and (d) the fourth group received questionnaires expressing similar opinions on the least important issues and dissimilar opinions on the most important.

Each subject indicated how much he liked the student who had filled out the questionnaire and how much he would enjoy working with the person in an experiment. In addition, the subject evaluated the other person on a number of other dimensions, such as intelligence and morality.

As we might expect, Byrne found that students liked the person who expressed views similar to their own very much more than the person who expressed dissimilar views. The person who expressed similar attitudes was also judged to be more intelligent, better informed, more moral, and better adjusted than the person with dissimilar attitudes.

With respect to the relative influence of similarity on important as opposed to unimportant issues, Byrne found that the person who agreed with the subject on important issues was liked more and was felt to be more moral and better adjusted than was the person who agreed with the subject only on unimportant issues. (Whether the other agreed on important or unimportant issues was found to have no effect on the subject's judgments as to the other's desirability as a work partner, intelligence, or knowledge of current events.)

Levinger and Breedlove (1966), also following Newcomb's formulation, tested an hypothesis similar to Byrne's. They reasoned that the more agreement on an issue facilitated the goals of the marital relationship, the more important agreement on the issue would be for marital satisfaction. (Marital satisfaction in their study, then, served as an indirect index of attraction between marital partners.)

To test their hypothesis, Levinger and Breedlove obtained from married couples a great deal of information concerning their own marriage and their attitudes toward marriage in general. Their data gave some weak, and statistically nonsignificant, support for the hypothesis that actual agreement and attraction are more highly correlated on attitudinal dimensions with implications for goal achievement in the marriage than on dimensions with lesser implications. Levinger and Breedlove attributed the lack of strong support for the hypothesis to the great difficulty involved in specifying precisely the instrumentality of agreement for each attitude.

It is evident from the body of research discussed in this section that similarity of attitude produces esteem with great consistency. Furthermore, since we know that esteem is generally reciprocated, we can see how more and more liking comes to be generated in interactions with those who hold attitudes similar to our own. When the other person also discovers that we hold attitudes similar to *his* own, his liking for us may be expected to increase. Knowledge that *he* likes *us* bolsters, in turn, our esteem for him, and in this way, as Newcomb has pointed out (1956), "attraction breeds attraction."

## SIMILARITY OF PERSONALITY

Perhaps the type of similarity which has received the most experimental attention has been that of personality. Here again, the hypothesis that friends *perceive* each other as being more similar in personality than do non-friends has been supported (e.g., Beier, Rossi, and Garfield, 1961; Broxton, 1963).

Do friends generally possess similar personality characteristics in fact? According to folk psychology, one's character *can* be judged by the company he keeps. Not only are similar individuals assumed to congregate ("Birds of a feather . . .") but individuals are assumed to become like their associates ("Keep not ill men company lest you increase the number"). Many a mother, anxious to save her innocent child's character—or at least his reputation—has forbidden him to keep bad company.

The method generally used to answer the question of whether or not friends actually do possess similar personality characteristics has been to compare an individual's personality test responses with the test responses of both his friends and non-friends. Reader and English (1947), for example, administered five personality tests to pairs of friends and pairs of non-friends and computed correlations between the pairs. These investigators found a significantly higher positive correlation between friends' personalities than between non-friends'.

One careful study examined not only the extent to which friends' and non-friends' descriptions of their own personalities were similar, but also the extent to which friends and non-friends were *viewed by others* acquainted with them as being similar in personality. Miller, Campbell, Twedt, and O'Connell (1966), collected their data from a number of residential groups including sororities, fraternities, and dormitories at Northwestern University. Residents in each group were requested to evaluate themselves and each of the people with whom they resided, on a number of personality traits. In addition, they were asked to indicate their five closest friends in the residential group.

An examination of the way the personalities of friends were described by their acquaintances revealed a stable relationship between friends' *reputations.* If, for example, one member of the friendship pair was viewed by other residents as conceited, his friend was likely to be viewed in the same way. Despite the evidence that others judged friends' personalities as being similar, the investigators found little similarity in the way friends described their *own* personalities.

How does one explain the fact that by reputation individuals are seen as being similar when according to their own descriptions they are not? After carefully considering a number of alternative explanations, the authors concluded that the reputational similarity of personality was most probably due to judgment error on the part of the acquaintances: "Those who are friends have been shown to be indeed similar on numerous other dimensions such as attitudes, socioeconomic class, religion, values, interests, etc. (Burgess and Wallin, 1953; Byrne and Blaylock, 1963; Lindzey and Borgatta, 1954; Richardson, 1939.) With so many dimensions on which true similarity exists, generalization of similarity to personality-trait dimensions could readily occur. The pairs who provided the reputations may have mistakenly rated those who navigate in space and time together and who tend to be similar on a variety of attitudinal, socioeconomic, interest and skill dimensions, as also similar on a variety of personality dimensions."*

A few investigators, such as Reader and English (1947) and Izard (1960a), have found positive correlations between friends' personality traits. Generally, however, positive correlations have not been obtained with the great regularity with which positive correlations between attitudinal similarity and attraction have been found. In addition, positive personality correlations are usually much lower than attitudinal correlations (cf. Richardson, 1939). This body of correlational data, then, prompts one to speculate that if personality similarity *is* a factor in attraction, it is perhaps a less important one than attitudinal similarity.

If it is true that friends tend to be at least somewhat more similar in personality than are non-friends, several questions arise:

1. Do friends *become* similar due to their association? It is easy to imagine, for example, that one might become much more aggressive if forced to interact continually with an aggressive person. It may be the case, as Plutarch claimed, that "if one lives with a lame person he will learn to limp."

---

*Miller, N., D. T. Campbell, H. Twedt, and E. J. O'Connell. "Similarity, contrast, and complementarity in friendship choice," *J. Pers. Soc. Psych.*, 1966, 3, p. 11.

2. Or, do people *select* each other as friends because they are similar?

3. Or, do individuals simply run into similar people for reasons that have nothing to do with their personal preferences? We discussed the importance of proximity as a determinant of interpersonal attraction in Chapter 4, and the evidence indicating that people are likely to choose their friends from those who just happen to be nearby. Due to a variety of reasons, it may very well be that people tend to be thrown together with those who possess similar personality characteristics. This might be particularly true in cases in which a particular type of personality is drawn to a certain type of occupation.

## Association as a Cause of Similarity

Let us now examine the plausibility of these three explanations for the similarities sometimes found to exist in friends' personalities.

With respect to the first possibility, if it is true that people become more similar due to their association, we should expect that resemblances in personality would become more pronounced between married couples the longer they have been married. The data concerning personality similarity between couples married for different time periods appear to be somewhat contradictory. Hunt (1935) found no correlation between length of time married and similarity in ranking of ideals; Hoffeditz (1934) found no evidence that resemblance on the personality traits of neurotic tendency, self-sufficiency and dominance increased with duration of marriage; and other studies (e.g., Schooley, 1936; Newcomb and Svehla, 1937) have obtained mixed results. Thus, it is not clear that frequent interaction produces personality similarity.

## Association as a Consequence of Similarity

The second notion, that people *select* their friends on the basis of similar personality characteristics, is a more popular explanation of the correlational data which indicate that friends have more similar personalities than non-friends.

Why should personality similarity be a factor in friendship formation? Why should we like those who possess personality characteristics similar to our own? Much of the research concerning personality similarity and attraction has been stimulated by a "theory of narcissism." It has been hypothesized that people like those who possess personality characteristics similar to their own due to the existence of strong narcissistic tendencies in people. These tendencies presumably lead "the individual to love in another person that which he sees in himself. That which is most like one's self is loved" (Reader and English, 1947, p. 216).

Few of the proponents of the narcissistic point of view elaborate upon why it is that it should be especially satisfying to behold personality characteristics in another which are similar to our own, and reference to a theory of narcissism does not make the personality similarity-attraction hypothesis self-evident. If we are irritable and excitable, is it especially satisfying to interact with another who possesses these same unfortunate traits? Is it rewarding to know that another possesses the same loathsome traits we do? Or is it the case that we wish to see only our good qualities reflected in another? But if we are fortunate enough to possess Job's patience and an ethereal calm, wouldn't it perhaps detract somewhat from our feelings of self-congratulation to interact with nuns, for example, who are trained to possess these qualities? Might we not prefer to interact with lesser mortals so that our goodness may shine in comparison?

It is not readily apparent why we should enjoy seeing our own personality characteristics reflected in others, but nevertheless, whether or not we do has been the focus of several studies. Izard (1960b) tested the hypothesis that his subjects would have significantly similar personality profiles, *prior* to acquaintance, to those people they liked, and less similarity to those people they disliked. Izard administered the *Edward Personal Preference Schedule* (EPPS) to an entire freshman class upon entering college. Six months later a number of female subjects in the group were given a sociometric form requiring them to list the three girls they liked most in their class and the three girls they liked least. Izard found that prior-to-acquaintance personality profiles were significantly similar for subjects and their most liked classmates, but not for subjects and those classmates they least liked.

## Association as a Consequence of Proximity

In interpreting the results of this study, we can be sure that the personality similarities found between friends existed *prior* to the friendship and were not a result of the friendship pairs becoming more similar through their interactions with one another. We cannot be completely certain, however, that personality similarity was the determining cause of friendship formation. We know that proximity is a factor in inducing interpersonal attraction. We do not know whether those of Izard's students who elected to take tapdancing, for example, to meet the physical education requirements, and who subsequently interacted with each other in dancing class, differed in personality from those who elected to learn judo or if those who enrolled in home economics differed in personality from those who enrolled in engineering. In short, we do not know the relationship between similarity of personality and proximity among Izard's subjects. Therefore, we cannot guess to what extent the "most liked" classmates were selected as friends simply due to the proximity factor rather than for reasons of personality similarity. On the basis of other investigations which have demonstrated that students who major in one area rather than another are likely to possess certain personality similarities (e.g., Goldschmid, 1967), we might speculate that proximity was at least partially a factor in producing Izard's results. To be certain that friends become friends because of personality similarity, frequency of interaction between similar and dissimilar personality types would need to be controlled.

Izard (1963) replicated his study with a similar sample of college freshmen and once again found a relationship between similarity of personality and sociometric choice. When, however, Izard applied his same experimental procedure to a different population, that of college seniors, the results failed to indicate any relationship between similarity of personality and interpersonal attraction. In interpreting his failure to replicate his results with the older subjects, Izard reasoned that it might have been due to an increased social and emotional maturity on the part of the seniors. He speculated that as one gains increased maturity, personality similarity may become a less important determinant of interpersonal attraction: "Perhaps the more 'mature' person has less need to see his personality characteristics reflected in his friends" (1963, p. 600).

Whether or not this is the true reason for the replication failure, Izard has some social support for the notion that a mentally healthy, mature person has less need to see his personality characteristics reflected in his friends. Maslow (1950), for example, has attempted to investigate, through questionnaire data and personal interviews, love in mentally healthy, "self-actualizing," people. It is Maslow's impression that in healthy people, homogamy is the rule only with respect to character traits such as honesty, sincerity, and so on: "In the more external and superficial characteristics . . . , the extent of homogamy seems to be significantly less than in average people. Self-actualizing people are not threatened by differences nor by strangeness. Indeed, they are rather intrigued than otherwise. They need familiar accents, clothes, food, customs, and ceremonies much less than do average people" (1953, p. 89).

If we can conclude that such traits measured by the EPPS as need for "autonomy," "change," or "exhibitionism" would be classified as superficial traits, Maslow would seem to agree with Izard that maturity decreases one's appreciation of personality uniformity.

In any case, whether or not people do select their friends on the basis of personality similarity is somewhat in doubt. In addition to Izard's report of his failure to replicate his finding with college seniors, several other investigators (e.g., Bonney, 1952, Hoffman, 1958) have concluded on the basis of their own investigations that personality similarity is not a sufficient condition for attraction to take place.

PERSONALITY SIMILARITY AND MARITAL HAPPINESS

It has been suggested that similarity of personality, like similarity in attitude, allows two people more easily to reward each other in marriage, and thus personality similarity leads to marital stability and happiness.

Research into the question of whether or not actual personality similarities between husbands and wives increase marital happiness has not been neglected.

Dymond (1954), for example, has found that, with respect to responses to *Minnesota Multiphasic Personality Inventory* (MMPI) items concerning interaction with others, happily married spouses were more similar to each other than unhappy spouses. More recently, Cattell and Nesselroade (1967) published similar findings. These authors investigated the degree to which similarity of personality, as measured by Cattell's 16 Personality Factor questionnaire, would be found in stable, vs. unstable, marriages. Their data provided a great deal of support for the hypothesis that similarity of personality is a characteristic of happily married couples.

## *Theory of Complementary Needs*

Researchers have considered not only the possibility that personality similarity would facilitate a rewarding marital relationship, and thus enhance marital love, but also the hypothesis that certain patterns of personality dissimilarity, rather than detracting from marital happiness, would actually enhance it. Undoubtedly the leading proponent of the point of view that certain dissimilarities in personality may actually facilitate interpersonal attraction has been Robert Winch. The basic hypothesis of Winch's "theory of complementary needs in mate selection" is that each individual chooses to mate with that person who is most likely to provide him or her with maximum need-gratification (1952). Noting that "love" is popularly regarded as the primary basis upon which people in our society select mates, Winch equates need-gratification with interpersonal attraction: ". . .'love' is defined as the experience of deriving gratification for important psychic needs from a peer-age person of the opposite sex, or the expectation of deriving such gratification" (Winch, Ktsanes, and Ktsanes, 1954, p. 241-242). While the lion's share of the research performed to test Winch's theory deals with engaged or married couples, Winch specifically states that the predictive domain of the theory includes attraction between same- and opposite-sexed friends as well as between engaged and married couples.

Winch and his associates theorize that the gratifications obtained when two individuals interact may be complementary in two different ways. Winch would label a need gratification pattern as an instance of Type I complementarity if the needs gratified in one person were of a different kind than those gratified in the other person. To illustrate this concept,

Winch states, "If A is highly ascendant, we should expect A to be more attracted maritally to B who is submissive than to C who, like A, is ascendant. If A is somewhat sadistic, we should expect A to be more attracted maritally to B who is somewhat masochistic than to C who is sadistic. If A is a succorant person, we should expect A to be attracted to nurturant B rather than to succorant C. And in each of these cases B should be reciprocally attracted to A" (Winch, Ktsanes and Ktsanes, 1954, p. 242).

Need gratification, according to Winch, may be complementary in another way: The needs of the one person may be the *same* as the needs of the other person, but the persons' needs may differ in intensity in such a way that both people are likely to experience need gratification in interaction with one another. If, for example, one individual has a high need for dominance and enjoys telling other people what to do, he might get along extremely well with a person who has a low need for dominance and who definitely wishes external direction for his activities. If the needs of two people are gratified in such a way, Winch would label their need gratification pattern as Type II complementarity.

What evidence is there that need complementarity is indeed a factor in interpersonal attraction? Winch and his associates examined the personality need patterns of 25 married couples, principally through interviews with these couples. To minimize the effect of marital interaction on the personalities of the spouses, all couples studied had been married less than two years and were childless. The investigators found that the number of correlations which were significant in the direction predicted by Winch's theory exceeded the number which could have been expected to occur by chance. On the basis of this evidence they concluded that ". . . persons like our subjects tend to select mates whose needs are complementary rather than similar to their own" (1954, pp. 245-248).

According to Winch's theory, need complementarity holds for engaged, as well as for married, couples. Bowerman and Day (1956) investigated the need-complementarity hypothesis with couples who were engaged or going steady. However, they were unable to replicate Winch's findings. Banta and Hetherington (1963) also investigated the role of complementarity and similarity of needs in the mate and friendship selections of college students. They found that the needs of engaged couples, for 8 of the 15 needs measured, were positively and significantly correlated. Thus, their data also fail to support the complementarity hypothesis, and in fact indicate a general preference in mate selection for a person with *similar*, rather than complementary needs.

Schellenberg and Bee (1960) obtained personality-need data from both married and courtship couples. Like Bowerman and Day, Schellenberg and Bee measured needs with the EPPS. The basic hypothesis of the Schellenberg and Bee study was that the need patterns of recently married couples and of courtship couples would be more *dissimilar* than would be expected by chance. The results of their study also failed to find support for the theory of complementary needs. Their results tended slightly in a direction of need similarity:

> In all, 69 of the 100 couples showed *positive* correlations of need patterns, including 73 percent of the married sample and 61 percent of the pre-married sample . . . The results for married couples differed significantly from chance; those of the pre-married group, though in the same direction of homogamy, failed to demonstrate statistical significance (1960, p. 115).

Some evidence supportive to the need-complementarity hypothesis was found by Kerckhoff and Davis (1962) who studied college couples who were seriously considering marriage. In this study, measures on need complementarity and consensus on family values were collected over a seven-month period. Correlations were then computed between these measures and the progress the couple made toward a permanent union with each other.

Kerckhoff and Davis hypothesized that degree of value consensus would be positively related to progress toward marriage and that degree of need complementarity would also be positively related to progress. Progress toward a permanent union was measured by asking couples if their relationship had changed in the past seven months (when they had first filled out questionnaires measuring needs and values). There were three possible responses to this question: "Yes, we are farther from being a permanent couple," "No, it is the same," "Yes, we are nearer to being a permanent couple."

All analyses took into consideration the fact that the couples had gone together for varying lengths of time before the study started. Couples who had gone together for 18 months or more were classified in one group, the "long-term" group. Those who had gone together less than 18 months were classified as "short-term."

The length of time subjects had gone together prior to the investigation was found to be a critical factor in determining the type of relationship found between the independent variables (need complimentarity and value consensus) and the dependent variable (progress toward permanence). Specifically, Kerckhoff and Davis found that value consensus was significantly related to progress for only the short-term couples; need complementarity was significantly related to progress only for the long-term couples.

These investigators interpreted their findings with reference to other research on mate selection. This research has indicated that a series of "filtering factors" operate in mate selection. Early in a relationship, social-status variables such as socioeconomic class, religion, and so on appear to have the major influence on whether or not a couple will continue to date. After the couple has been going together a little longer, consensus on values becomes an important determinant of whether or not the relationship will continue. Only very late in the relationship does need complementarity become important.

The Kerckhoff-Davis research, in any event, gives support both to similarity and to complementarity theories, and provides some insight into how these two factors may operate in mate selection.

We have seen that the evidence for the Winch hypothesis, that friends and courtship couples will select one another on the basis of need complementarity, is very weak.

In addition to the negative findings previously mentioned, others have found little or no support for the hypothesis. Murstein (1961) studied couples married for varying lengths of time. A number of personality measures, including the EPPS, were administered to 20 newlywed couples and 40 married couples. The examination of personality-need patterns tended to favor a homogamous theory of need-pattern choice for the couples who had been married for some period of time. The evidence obtained from the newlyweds was entirely inconclusive in that neither the homogamous nor the need-complementarity theory of marital choice was supported.

Negative results for need complementarity were also obtained by Becker (1964) who examined the relationship between authoritarianism and the need for dominance and deference. The theory of need complementarity would predict that people who are high in authoritarianism would be likely to choose mates who are low in the need for dominance and deference. No such relationship was evident in the data.

The major evidence, then, supporting the need-complementarity hypothesis appears to be Winch's original data. Although the analysis of these data have been severely criticized on methodological grounds (e.g., Tharp, 1963), it is observed by Levinger (1964) that "many of the most productive human relationships are complementary ones: male and female in the sex act, seller and buyer in the exchange, and so forth" (p. 164). Since the complementary-need hypothesis is basically so reasonable, Levinger feels that lack of supporting evidence may be due to difficulties in the conceptualization of the hypothesis. In particular, Levinger cites the lack of explicit theoretical basis for deciding beforehand which needs will be complementary with which others, and which will not.

In addition, Levinger presents a second possible explanation for some of the negative findings of the need-complementarity studies. Specifically, he states that an implicit assumption has been that need-fit pertains primarily to the marital relationship itself. However, each marriage partner interacts not only with his spouse but with many others. Because both partners are simultaneously involved with other people, there are probably many substitute sources which can gratify each person's needs. The man whose need for dominance is frustrated at home, for example, may go to work and bully his secretary.

Levinger notes that the conceptual distinction between internal and external sources of need satisfaction has been ignored operationally by such researchers as Bowerman and Day and Schellenberg and Bee. In their studies, they used the EPPS to measure marital needs, although this instrument was designed to measure needs in the global environment. Levinger concludes that:

> Their negative findings merely demonstrate, therefore, that marriage partners do not show any consistent correlation between such *general* needs. These studies can hardly claim to test the complementarity of these needs in the specific *marriage* situation (1964, p. 156).

To support this point Levinger refers to a study conducted by Katz, Glucksberg, and Krauss (1960) which examined need satisfaction and EPPS scores in married couples. These investigators rewrote EPPS items describing general need for Nurturance and for Succorance so that they pertained specifically to the marital situation. While their results were generally not supportive of the need-complementarity hypothesis, their most significant evidence of complementarity in need gratification was found for those needs measured in such a way as to be specifically relevant to marital interaction. Levinger concludes that "Until investigators take account of this issue more directly in their measurement of specific needs, there will be no further evidence to support the original hypothesis by Winch and his colleagues" (1964, p. 156).

Quite a different possible explanation of the frequent failure to find support for the need-complementarity hypothesis has been advanced by Rosow (1957). He has criticized Winch's approach of dealing with an individual's personality needs in a discrete and independent fashion. He has suggested that the need-complementarity hypothesis might be more likely to be confirmed if need complementarity were analyzed in a framework of more global personality type. Investigators who have used such a holistic approach in analyzing Winch's original data (e.g., Ktsanes, 1955; Roos, 1956) have supported the generalization regarding dissimilar need patterns of spouses.

## The Need Completion Principle

An hypothesis somewhat similar to the need-complementarity hypothesis has been investigated by Cattell and Nesselroade (1967). Cattell has reasoned that choice in friendship and in marriage may be directed by

> a desire to possess characteristics (by sharing them in the possessed partner) which are felt by the individual to be necessary to his self-concept or to his or her social and general life adjustment in marriage ... For example, a socially awkward person might especially value a partner who is socially adroit and poised (1967, p. 351).

The completion principle differs somewhat from the complementary-need hypothesis. The completion principle is not particularly concerned with the consequences of the individual's interactions. In addition, the completion principle involves the matter of personal desirability to a greater extent than does the need-complementarity principle. The principle ". . . states that every person tends to seek in a partner much the same set of desirables—good looks, intelligence, emotional stability, etc.—but more so to the extent that he or she lacks them" (1967, p. 356).

This interesting notion has also been advanced, though in slightly different terms, by several psychoanalytic theorists. Theodor Reik, for example, in discussing the origin and nature of romantic love, dismisses quickly the similarity notion:

> As long as one person meets another and does not see him as a different individual with a different make-up, love is psychologically not possible. The difference has to be felt, although it need not become conscious. If the object is exactly like me, where is the necessity to love him? If the other person is precisely as I am, where is the possibility of loving him or her—except in a psychoanalytical theory that we love only ourselves in the other? [Reik persuasively goes on to reject this theory (1944, p. xiv-xv).]

Reik then proceeds to argue that we tend to fall in love with those who possess qualities of which we are envious.

Cattell and Nesselroade found little supporting evidence for the completion principle in an examination of the personality responses of stably and unstably married couples. Nevertheless, this hypothesis is an interesting one and some supportive evidence for it is provided by studies in which individuals were asked to describe their friends. When individuals perceived that their friends were different from themselves, the difference usually was of a specific type. The dissimilar friend was perceived to possess traits which the individual admired, and wished he possessed, but which he felt he lacked. (See Reader and English, 1947; Thompson and Nishimura, 1952; Lundy, Katkovsky, Cromwell and Shoemaker, 1955; O'Connor, 1956; and Beier, Rossi and Garfield, 1961.

Let us discuss the Beier, Rossi and Garfield (1961) study in some detail. Subjects in this experiment completed the *Minnesota Multiphasic Personality Inventory* under three sets of instructions. They first filled out the MMPI as they normally would. They then tried to guess how their best friend would answer the items. Finally, they tried to guess how their most disliked acquaintance would answer the items.

Beier *et al.* predicted that individuals would (1) project more of their own personal characteristics on friends than on those they disliked; (2) project more socially approved characteristics on friends than they attributed to themselves; and (3) project more socially disapproved characteristics on disliked persons than they attributed to themselves. The data confirmed all three hypotheses. Subjects tended to assume that their friends were psychologically stronger and better adjusted than they were themselves. "The friend as compared with the self is seen as more social, less depressed, less susceptible to moods, less concerned with bodily functions, less incapacitated by feelings of inadequacy, and generally more active and realistic than oneself. If the individual doing the rating is a male, he sees his male friend as being more interested in masculine activities than himself" (1961, p. 7). Similarly, subjects tended to perceive that their enemies were much more psychologically maladjusted than they were. "The disliked person as compared to the self is seen as being more impulsive, more suspicious of others, with more idiosyncratic ideas, and also with more aggressiveness. The non-friend was attributed an excess of almost all the characteristics tapped by the MMPI, i.e., impulsiveness, moodiness, concern with bodily functions, feelings of inadequacy, depression, social isolation, idiosyncratic ideas, and manic activity" (1961, p. 7).

The finding that one tends to suspect the sanity of those people he dislikes can be supported by everyday observation. Observe the "Letters to the Editor" column in your daily newspaper for a short period. You will soon notice that irate readers on both sides of an issue manage to find clear evidence that their opponents are deranged. The opposition appears to have equal confidence that their supporters possess excellent mental health.

Even psychiatrists appear not to be immune to the temptation to assume that those who agree with them on various issues must be mentally healthier than are those who do not happen to share their views. At the time of the 1964 presidential election, *Fact* magazine reported the results of a poll of 12,356 psychiatrists. The poll was designed to assess whether or not Barry Goldwater, the Republican candidate for president, was "psychologically fit" to serve as president. In violation of all reasonable standards, almost half of the psychiatrists who responded—most of whom had never even spoken to Mr. Goldwater, much less examined him—willingly provided their opinion that Mr. Goldwater's state of mental health left much to be desired. He was diagnosed as a "dangerous compensated schizophrenic," a "paranoid," a "severe obsessive-compulsive neurotic," etc. One psychiatrist felt so strongly about his mail-order diagnosis of Goldwater as a "dangerous lunatic" that he felt compelled to add: "Any psychiatrist who does not agree with the above is himself psychologically unfit to be a psychiatrist." Needless to say, one can be fairly confident that these same psychiatrists were overwhelmingly for the Democratic candidate.

### Correlation in Mental Health

Before leaving our discussion of the role of personality similarities and dissimilarities in interpersonal attraction, we should perhaps note that among clinicians who deal intimately with unhappy human beings, including those enmeshed in marital problems, there is rather widespread agreement that heterosexual attraction quite frequently takes place on the basis of similarity with respect to the general personality characteristic of neuroticism. Perhaps Edmund Bergler, the psychoanalyst, presents the case most strongly: "All stories about a normal woman who becomes the prey of a neurotic man, and vice versa, or a normal man who falls in love with a highly neurotic woman, are literary fairy tales. Real life is less romantic; two neurotics look for each other with uncanny regularity. Nothing is left to chance, as far as emotional attachments are concerned" (1948, p. 11).

In addition to the anecdotal and experimental data upon which many clinical psychologists and psychiatrists have advanced this point of view, there exists some recent, relatively "harder," data in support of the proposition that neurotics tend to marry neurotics: Murstein (1967) administered the MMPI to 99 couples who were either engaged or going steady. Some of the variables subsequently examined were anxiety, ego strength, and repression; in addition a global assessment of their entire MMPI responses was rendered by a clinician. Six months later these couples were requested to indicate on a questionnaire whether or not they had progressed in their courtship. Murstein found that his couples showed a significant correlation in mental health and, further, that couples similar in mental health progressed further in courtship than dissimilar couples.

While clinicians agree that similarity in terms of mental health appears to be a factor in mate selection, they also appear to agree that the basis of this global similarity is neurotic need-complementarity. The lack of data supporting this hypothesis, and possible reasons for it, has been previously mentioned.

## SIMILARITY ALONG OTHER DIMENSIONS

While the bulk of the similarity-attraction research has focused upon similarities of personality and of attitude, similarity along other dimensions—such as intelligence and social characteristics—has been investigated as well.

Some attempt, for example, has been made to investigate the degree to which physical similarities are related to attraction. Unfortunately, most of these studies are correlational, and interpretation of the cause and effect relationships involved are difficult. Again, the existence of attraction has been assumed from evidence that a couple is either engaged or married.

### *Physical Characteristics*

Folklore contains many hypotheses associated with the question of whether or not similarities or dissimilarities in physical appearance enhance or lessen attraction possibilities. Harris, writing in 1912, states some common beliefs: "Weak or little men have a decided inclination for strong or big women, and strong or big women for weak or little men. Blondes prefer dark persons or brunettes; snub-nosed, hook-nosed; persons with excessively thin, long bodies and limbs, those who are stumpy and short, and so on!" (p. 478). While there does not appear to be any research which demonstrates that a person tends to prefer those who possess noses disparate from his own, there is evidence that, at least as far as marital selection is concerned, little men evidently do not have an inclination for large women. Correlations between the stature of husbands and wives are generally positive: short men tend to marry short women (e.g., Pearson and Lee, 1903).

There does appear to be some tendency for those with physical defects to marry those possessing like defects. This appears to be especially true with respect to deafness. Harris, for example, states that "assortative mating for deafness is more nearly perfect than for any other known character" (1912, p. 484). It is interesting that the fact that deaf people do tend to marry one another so impressed Alexander Graham Bell (1883) that he felt compelled to point out the grave consequences of this tendency in an article entitled "Upon the Formation of a Deaf Variety of the Human Race."

There are probably many reasons for the tendency of those who possess physical defects to marry one another. Perhaps the most compelling explanation of the relationship is that those who possess a defect tend to be more often in proximity with one another than those without. It is interesting, nevertheless, that some similarities of defect between people may produce happier relationships than if one member of the pair does not possess the defect. Harris reports data collected by Fay (1898) which indicate that marriages in which both members are deaf are happier than those in which only one is afflicted. The divorce and separation rate of marriages in which both partners are deaf is much less than that for marriages in which only one partner is deaf.

### Intelligence and Education

A great deal of attention has been given to the relationship between similarity of intelligence level and attraction. The correlations obtained between intelligence of husbands and wives have been approximately of the magnitude +.40 (e.g., Jones, 1929; Reed and Reed, 1965). Intelligence correlations taken between friends are also positive, but tend to be lower (cf. Richardson, 1939). Again these correlational data may be easily explained in terms of the fact that people of like intelligence are much more likely to be thrown together than people of unlike intelligence. It would be interesting, however, to know whether or not the factor of intelligence does operate independently as a determinant of interpersonal attraction. Is intelligence a socially desirable characteristic which is found attractive even by those of low intelligence, or is it the case that a person of low intelligence can better reward another person of low intelligence than can a person of high intelligence? This last possibility may also underlie the correlations obtained between intelligence and attraction.

As might be expected, uniformly high correlations have been obtained between husbands and wives on the variable of educational attainment (Garrison, Anderson, and Reed, 1968). Again, it is clear that people of like educational level interact with each other more often than those of unlike level. But, in addition, similarity of educational attainment subsumes many cultural and attitudinal similarities which individuals may find attractive in each other.

### Social Characteristics

One important study in investigating similarity of engaged couples along various social dimensions was conducted by Burgess and Wallin (1943). On almost every characteristic investigated by Burgess and Wallin there was found evidence of positive correlation, evidence of similarity, between the engaged couples. Similarity was found with respect to (a) family background, including place lived in childhood, educational level, nativity, income and social status of parents; (b) religious affiliation; (c) types of family relationship, including happiness of parents' marriage, attitude toward the father when a child, and sex of siblings; (d) social participation, including the tendency to be a lone wolf rather than socially gregarious, leisure time preference ("stay at home" *vs.* "on the go"), drinking habits, smoking habits, number of friends of same sex, as well as opposite sex, and so on.

Similarity among the couples was found also with respect to their courtship behavior. Variables here included whether or not the person had been previously engaged and the number of people he had gone with steadily. A similarity of attitude toward marriage was also found among couples, but this, of course, may have come about through their interaction with one another. Burgess and Wallin, then, present overwhelming evidence that like tends to marry like on the basis of social characteristics.

# CHAPTER SEVEN

# Rewards Others Provide:
# Cooperation vs. Competition

Many times people do not reward or punish us directly; rather, they are instrumental either in helping us obtain desired goals or in blocking our progress toward need gratification. As we might expect, there is a great deal of evidence which indicates that we tend to like those who cooperate with us in our attempts to obtain rewards for ourselves (e.g., Berkowitz and Daniels, 1963; Goranson and Berkowitz, 1966). There is also evidence that we tend to dislike those who frustrate our attempts to obtain reward, whether they do so because of maliciousness or because they find themselves competing against us for rewards (e.g., Burnstein and Worchel, 1962).

## COOPERATION AND COMPETITION

Perhaps the most interesting and best known studies which have examined the relationship between cooperation, competition, and interpersonal attraction have been performed under the direction of Muzafer Sherif (e.g., Sherif, Harvey, White, Hood and Sherif, 1961). Subjects in this series of field experiments were boys of about twelve years of age who attended a summer camp run by the experimenters. All boys were strangers to one another prior to attending camp, and there were, therefore, no established friendships between them. The camps were ostensibly set up to study "camping methods and group living in general." In actuality, the investigators were primarily interested in studying intergroup relations, and especially the effectiveness of various techniques for reducing hostility between groups. The camp setting, isolated from outside influences, afforded the experimenters a unique opportunity to manipulate the conditions and circumstances of interaction between the camp members. Such control was necessary for the creation of hostility between campers, and for subsequent examination of the efficacy of various hostility-reduction techniques.

To create intergroup hostility, it was first necessary for the experimenters to divide up the campers into groups and to instill in each group an *esprit de corps.* For this reason, the boys within each camp were assigned to one of two separate living groups, each of which was given a name (e.g., "Bull Dogs" and "Red Devils"). In an attempt to assure that a feeling of "we-ness" would develop within each group, the daily activities of each living group were planned in such a way that interdependent, coordinated activity among the members was necessary to the achievement of desirable goals. The food, for example, was unprepared. In order to eat, coordinated activity such as building a fire, proportioning the food, and so on, was required.

### Development of Antagonism

Following the successful development within the camp of two "in-groups," characterized by mutual good feeling between in-group members, the experimenters then attempted to induce animosity between the in-groups. The "Bull Dogs" and "Red Devils," for example, were often brought together to participate in competitive, mutually frustrating, activities in which the securing of rewards by one group necessarily frustrated the obtaining of rewards by the other group. The effects of the competitive games were not immediate at first. Initial good sportsmanship on the part of both groups resulted in the winning group spontaneously giving a cheer for the losers and the losers responding with a cheer for the winners. Fortunately for the experimenters, however, the effects of competition evidenced themselves in time: "... as the series of contests progressed, this cheer changed from '2-4-6-8, who do we appreciate,' followed by the name of the other group, to '2-4-6-8, who do we appreci*hate*' " (Sherif and Sherif, 1956, p. 294).

Winning points could be accumulated in the series of competitive games and camp contests, and in one camp the series culminated in the award of a prize to the members of the winning group, the "Bull Dogs." By this time, the hostility of the "Red Devils" toward the "Bull Dogs" was not restricted to a subtle change in the wording of a cheer. The "Bull Dogs" were often accused of indulging in foul play during the contests and were frequently the targets of other verbal abuse.

The series of competitive games and the awarding of the prize was followed by plans for a party which, the "Bull Dogs" and "Red Devils" were told, would help them rid themselves of all bad feeling toward the other group. Both groups agreed to attend the party. Although it had been represented as a peacemaking party, the experimenters were not through with their tension-creating manipulations. They placed the party refreshments on a table in such a way that half looked delicious and appetizing and the other half appeared crushed and unappealing. The experimenters detonated this volatile situation by contriving for the "Red Devils" to arrive at the party first. The experimenters were not disappointed when nature took its course and the "Red Devils" grabbed the good half of the refreshments and sat down to enjoy them. The result was better than even Mephistopheles could have anticipated.

> When the 'Bull Dogs' arrived a short time later and saw the sorry-looking refreshments left, they immediately protested. The 'Red Devils' justified their actions with 'first come, first served,' which became the standardized justification for all 'Red Devils.' The 'Bull Dogs' proceeded to eat their refreshments, hurling taunts, insults, and names at the 'Red Devils.' Particularly common was the term 'pigs.' Among the names used by most 'Bull Dogs' for 'Red Devils' on this and later occasions were 'pigs,' 'dirty bums' or 'red bums,' 'jerks,' and several more objectionable terms.

> The next morning the 'Red Devils' retaliated by deliberately dirtying their breakfast table to make K.P. duty harder for the 'Bull Dogs.' Upon seeing the dirty table, the 'Bull Dogs' decided to mess it up further and leave it. All 'Bull Dogs' joined in by smearing the table with cocoa, sugar, syrup, and the like, and leaving it alive with bees and wasps. The 'Bull Dogs' hung the walls with threatening and derogatory posters against the 'Red Devils.'

> At lunch that day the hostility between the groups increased to such a point throughout the meal that they soon were lined up on opposite sides of the mess hall calling names and then throwing food, cups, tableware, etc. The fight was broken up. Neither group was sure who started the fight, but each was sure it was someone in the *other* group.*

Given such a description, it seems superfluous to report the results of a sociometric test which was administered by the experimenters to see whether or not they had been successful in creating friendship bonds within each in-group and animosity toward members of the out-group. Suffice it to say that few "Red Devils" counted any "Bull Dogs" among their bosom buddies.

### Reduction of Hostility

After the successful creation of intergroup hostility in their series of field experiments, the experimenters proceeded to investigate the effectiveness of various hostility-reduction techniques.

---

*Sherif, M. and L. W. Sherif. *An Outline of Social Psychology* (rev. ed.). New York: Harper and Row, 1956, p. 296.

It will be recalled that Lott and Lott (1961) found support for the hypothesis that the response to a reward may become conditioned to persons present at the time of the rewarding experience and may lead to increased esteem for them. To investigate the efficacy of this approach to reducing hostility between groups, members of rival groups were given an opportunity to make social contact with each other in pleasant situations. The consequences of the use of this approach demonstrate the distance which sometimes exists between the laboratory and field situations:

> There were seven different contact situations, including eating together in the same dining room, watching a movie together, and shooting firecrackers in the same area. These contact situations had no effect in reducing intergroup friction. If anything they were utilized by members of both groups as opportunities for further name-calling and conflict. For example, they used mealtimes in the same place for 'garbage fights,' throwing mashed potatoes, left-overs, bottle caps, and the like, accompanied by the exchange of derogatory names.*

The experimenters concluded that contact between groups does not in itself produce a decrease in an existing state of intergroup tension. They also specifically note that their results place doubt upon the hypothesis that the reward of engaging in a pleasant activity will become conditioned to others who are in the immediate vicinity. It should be observed, however, that the "pleasant activities" Sherif and Sherif describe actually are quite compli-cated, as far as an analysis of the reinforcements involved is concerned. Though the situations were intended to be rewarding experiences which the rival groups would share, it is possible that the hostile behavior of the rival groups (i.e., name-calling, etc.) made the shared situations fairly unpleasant. If this were the case, rival groups were sharing unpleasant, rather than pleasant experiences. On the other hand, it is possible that the "garbage fights," etc. were themselves additional sources of fun. If this were the case, perhaps the boys were inadvertently being rewarded *for* hostile behavior toward the out-group. Such reward would of course be expected to *increase* the boys' antagonism toward the out-group. In any case, the first technique the authors tried, having the boys share an experience they hoped would be pleasant, did not decrease intergroup tension.

Since cooperation toward common goals had been effective in forming the two in-groups originally, the experimenters reasoned that they might reduce hostility, and create one large in-group from the two smaller in-groups, by bringing both groups together in cooperative situations. One such situation involved a camp-wide softball game in which selected members of both groups competed against an outside group of boys from a nearby town. The "common enemy" approach was found to be effective in reducing the hostility between campers. The experimenters, however, did

---

*Ibid.*, p. 318.

not pursue this technique further since, although it reduced hostility between the smaller groups, it eventually would lead to an equal or greater amount of hostility between the larger group units. The experimenters were not interested in transferring intergroup hostility from one group to another, but rather in discovering how to *eliminate* intergroup hostility.

Thus the effect of cooperative situations, which did not involve a human common enemy, was also investigated. Camp activities and events were planned in such a way that desirable goals could not be achieved by the efforts of one in-group alone; they could only be achieved if members of both groups cooperated toward the common goal. One goal involved repairing the water-supply system which the experimenters had earlier sabotaged. Another was cooperating together to obtain money to secure a movie that both groups wanted to see. And still another involved getting a truck to move, which had suddenly broken down on its way to bring food for a camp-out. The campers achieved all goals by cooperative activity.

After the campers had participated in these cooperative activities, a sociometric test was administered to group members. The results clearly revealed that attitudes toward members of the out-group had changed. Although friendship choices were primarily within each in-group, choices of out-group members as friends had increased. In addition to the increased tendency to choose out-group members as friends, the experimenters found a significant reduction in the number of rejections of members of the out-group as disliked persons.

Why should we like those with whom we cooperate? There are a number of possible explanations for these findings. One possibility, of course, is simply that through conditioning, as Lott and Lott suggest, one comes to like those who are present at the time of reward. If this is the only reason cooperation is effective in increasing esteem, then cooperation should create attraction between cooperating people only if the cooperative effort culminates in reward.

Other theorists would argue that cooperative efforts which fail may also produce increased interpersonal attraction. Cooperation ordinarily implies that at least two people are putting forth some effort to obtain a goal. If the cooperative effort fails, and the worked-for reward is not forthcoming, the participants may experience dissonance. Several experimenters have demonstrated that an individual who expends a great deal of effort and then reaps no benefit may justify his behavior to himself (and reduce his dissonance) by increasing his appreciation for various other aspects of the effort situations (e.g., Aronson and Mills, 1959). Since other cooperating people are an extremely salient aspect of an unfruitful cooperative situation, one might expect that individuals whose cooperative efforts fail could justify their efforts by exaggerating other benefits associated with the situation— e.g., the development of friendships. A man who works two years on a novel and then finds that no one will publish it may decide that the project nevertheless had some merit because it gave him the chance to spend time with his secretary.

Cooperation may, of course, promote liking even before it is known whether the cooperative effort will result in success or failure. The reader will recall from the discussion of research in Chapter 4 that Heider would expect individuals in close proximity to one another, and who are working on a similar project, to perceive themselves as a "unit." Individuals have been found to increase their liking for those they perceive as being in a unit relationship with themselves. (See Berscheid, Boye and Darley, 1968.)

## FRUSTRATION AND AGGRESSION

It seems evident from the evidence presented in the preceding section that individuals tend to like those with whom they cooperate. In this section we will see that the complement of this principle also appears to be true: individuals tend to dislike those who frustrate their attempts to secure desired goals.

In their book *Frustration and Aggression,* Dollard *et al.* (1939) provide a theoretical framework which enables one to predict the effect frustration will have on interpersonal attraction. In order to understand the research which has been conducted to test the relationships between frustration and aggression, we must first understand how these authors define the terms "frustration" and "aggression." Frustration is defined as "an interference with the occurrence of an instigated goal response at its proper time in the behavior sequence" (p. 7). In other words, a "frustration" is a condition or event which prevents an individual who has begun progressing towards a goal, from reaching that goal. Aggression is defined as "any sequence of behavior, the goal response to which is the injury of the person toward whom it is directed" (p. 9). In other words, a person is aggressing if, and only if, by his fantasies, plans, or actions he intends to injure another.

Dollard *et al.* contend that frustration is a necessary and sufficient condition for aggression. Specifically, they state "Aggression is always a consequence of frustration . . ." and ". . . whenever frustration occurs, aggression of some kind and of some degree will inevitably result" (p. 1). In arguing that a frustrated individual always reacts with aggression, the authors did not overlook the fact that human beings often have to learn to suppress and restrain overt aggressive reactions. They simply argue that even though an individual may restrain himself from certain aggressive responses, he will express his aggression in some other form. They argue, "It has been found that although these reactions may be temporarily compressed, delayed, disguised, displaced or otherwise deflected from their immediate and logical goal, they are not destroyed" (p. 2).

Some critics have quarrelled with the strong statement that frustration is a necessary and sufficient condition for aggression. (For example, see Bandura and Walters (1963) and Miller (1941) for an elucidation of the various objections that have been raised.) Though many theorists would agree that the connection between frustration and aggression is not as inevitable as Dollard *et al.* indicate, they would also probably agree that frustrated individuals are in general more likely to aggress against others than are non-frustrated individuals. Much experimental research supports this point of view. Relevant research has been conducted by Berkowitz (1965); Berkowitz and Green (1962); Berkowitz and Holmes (1960); Berkowitz and Rawlings (1963); Burnstein and Worchel (1962); Elbert and Ulrich, cited in Ulrich, 1966, p. 660; Hamblin (1958); Hamblin, Bridger, Day, and Yancey (1963); Hokanson (1961); Horwitz (1958); and Mallick and McCandless (1966).

### What Determines How Frustrating an Experience Is?

The Yale group hypothesizes that "the strength of instigation to aggression varies directly with the amount of frustration" (p. 28). This means that the more an individual is frustrated, the more aggressive he will tend to be. But what determines how frustrated an individual is? According to the authors, the amount of frustration one experiences, and thus the strength of one's instigation to aggress, is a positive function of three factors: (1) "the strength of the instigation to the frustrated response"; (2) "the number of frustrated response-sequences"; and (3) "the degree of interference with the frustrated response."

1. The notion that the stronger a drive one thwarts, the more frustrated the thwarted individual will be, and thus the more aggression he will demonstrate, receives some support from an experiment conducted by Sears and Sears (cited in Dollard *et al.*, 1939, pp. 28-29.) This proposition makes intuitive sense. We are undoubtedly more frustrated when a talkative salesman corners us on our way to dinner than when on our way to a boring lecture.

2. In arguing that frustration is a positive function of the number of frustrated response-sequences, the authors are merely observing that frustration is cumulative. They are pointing out that relatively minor frustrations, when close together in time, will produce an aggressive response greater in strength than would be expected from one minor frustrating event alone. There is only anecdotal evidence for this proposition. For example, they report that a man who had previously been a willing subject in several very trying and arduous experiments, when asked to free-associate to 50 words, lost his temper. This last irritation was obviously "the straw that broke the camel's back."

3. The notion that the more one interferes with an individual's progress toward a goal response, the more frustrated and aggressive the thwarted individual will be, has received support from several correlational studies which have gained widespread attention because the variables they utilize have great social significance. For example, Hovland and Sears (1940) have argued that "aggressive acts should be more numerous during years of depression than during years of prosperity," since during an economic depression many of an individual's needs are thwarted. The worse the economic conditions are, the less money individuals have to buy the things that they need, and the more frustrated they should be. Hovland and Sears tested the speculation that there would be a negative correlation between economic prosperity and group aggression. As an index of economic prosperity the authors chose the annual per-acre value of cotton in fourteen Southern states for the years 1882-1930. As a measure of aggression they chose the number of lynchings in these same fourteen states during the same period. The data revealed that during the period when economic prosperity was steadily increasing (from 1882-1930), the number of lynchings steadily decreased, as the authors expected. The authors also made a more crucial test of their hypothesis. They considered not just the general upward or downward trends of prosperity and lynchings, but also the effect that unexpected recessions or prosperity had on aggression. They first calculated the extent to which economic conditions or lynching frequencies deviated from the general trend lines. Then they correlated these corrected scores. The authors found that the correlation between the value of cotton and the total number of lynchings was $-.63$. Thomas (1925) also found a relationship between frustration and aggression. He found that economic indices and "property crimes with violence" were correlated $-.44$.

Hovland and Sears (1940, pp. 308-309) report additional intriguing evidence in support of the frustration-aggression hypothesis. They report that Marshall (1927) found that frustration may produce aggression toward politicians as well as toward Negroes. Writing during a period in which the country was more rural and more dependent on farming than it is today, Marshall noted that politicians were regularly voted out of office following periods of deficient rainfall. He said:

> Over a sixty-year period, in seven cases out of eight (Presidential elections) when the rainfall was greater than normal, the party in power, regardless of which one it was, continued to stay in power. On the other hand, in six cases out of seven when the rainfall was less than normal, a new swarm of political parasites descended on Washington.

It might be noted that according to the Dollard *et al.* theory, deprivation, in and of itself, is not synomyous with "frustration." It is only when an act "interferes with an instigated goal response"—when an act interrupts an individual's progress toward a goal, or blocks the rewards that an individual has come to expect—that frustration exists and aggression should occur. This point has some interesting ramifications.

Berkowitz (1969), after pointing out that frustration exists only when an individual's anticipatory goal responses (or expectations) are prevented from reaching fulfillment, notes

> the politico-social counterpart of this formulation is obvious; the phrase 'revolution of rising expectations' refers to just this conception of frustration. Poverty-stricken groups who had never dreamed of having automobiles, washing-machines, or new homes are not frustrated because they had been deprived of these things; they are frustrated only after they had begun to hope. If they had dared to think they might get these objects and had anticipated their satisfactions, the inability to fulfill their anticipations is a frustration. Privations in themselves are much less likely to breed violence than are the dashing of hopes.

> James Davies (1962) has employed this type of reasoning in his theory of revolutions. The American, French, and Russian Revolutions did not arise because these people were subjected to prolonged, severe hardships, Davies suggested. In each of these revolutions, and others as well, the established order was overthrown when a sudden, sharp socioeconomic decline abruptly thwarted the hopes and expectations that had begun to develop in the course of gradually improving conditions.*

## The Inhibition of Aggressive Acts

Obviously an individual does not express overt aggression every time he is frustrated. We can probably all agree that if a student, who was speeding to a final exam, was stopped by a policeman and given a ticket and a long lecture on reckless driving, the student would be frustrated. We can also probably agree, however, that the probabilities are very low that the student would hit the policeman or run him over with his car, or even call the policeman names. The reason that the student would not respond with overt aggression is that he is afraid that he will be punished if he does so.

Dollard and his colleagues (1939) pointed out that anticipated punishment would inhibit overt aggression. They propose that "the strength of inhibition of any act of aggression varies positively with the amount of punishment anticipated to be a consequence of that act" (p. 33). The authors assumed that *specific* aggressive acts which are followed by punishment would come to be suppressed. They were *not* implying that an

---

*Berkowitz, L. *Roots of Aggression: A Re-examination of the Frustration-Aggression Hypothesis.* New York: Atherton Press, 1969.

individual punished for aggression learns never to be aggressive, but rather that he learns to express his aggression in other forms (say, in aggressive fantasies).

The fact that anticipated punishment merely causes frustrated individuals to suppress their aggressive responses, and does not completely eliminate all aggression, is evident. On occasion, when the threat of possible punishment for antisocial behavior is removed, one is surprised to find that an individual whom he had always categorized as mild-mannered and civilized emerges as a pugnacious combatant. When placed in a punishment-free environment, the Walter Mitty's of the world, previously forced to confine their aggression to fantasy, are given the opportunity to live their aggressive dreams. There is some research to support the observation that normally staid individuals will act in more socially unacceptable ways when placed in a punishment-free environment than they will in their normal environments. It has often been noted that in a mob individuals often feel anonymous and thus safe from retribution for their actions. Festinger, Pepitone, and Newcomb (1952) noted that conservative American Legionnaires have been known to turn into boisterous and riotous individuals at their national conventions. The conventioneers are away from their homes, in a city where nobody knows them, and they are part of a large, anonymous, and perceptually homogenous group. For the first time many of them may feel safe to indulge in activities that they would normally have to suppress. Festinger *et al.* labeled this process of losing identity "deindividuation." Their research supported the notion that individuals will express more overt aggression if others in the group are not able to easily identify them, than they normally would.

## The Direction of Aggression

Much experimental work has focused on the direction that aggressive responses will take. The authors of *Frustration and Aggression* argued that the most satisfying target for aggression is the frustrating agent himself (p. 40).

It is not always possible to aggress against the frustrating agent, however. Sometimes a frustrated person is unable to identify the source of his frustration. Sometimes it is socially inappropriate for one to aggress against his frustrator. (It is unacceptable to hit the octogenarian wearing glasses, a hearing aid, and braces who accidentally trips over your foot.) Sometimes one is afraid to aggress against his frustrator. Often one is weaker than his frustrator. For example, a child is often frustrated by his parents. He soon learns, however, that if he aggresses directly against the source of the frustration he will be punished. "Honor thy father and thy mother" is a rule congenial to parents, and it is a rule that they generally take the trouble to enforce.

When an individual is inhibited from aggressing directly against the source of his frustration, he has a tendency to perform less direct acts of aggression—to "displace" his aggression by directing it towards someone or something which is not responsible for his frustration. That individuals do often displace their aggression is obvious. The man who is frustrated at the office is afraid to yell at his boss so he yells at his wife—she in turn may pick on the children.

It has often been proposed that individuals who are unable or afraid to aggress directly against their frustrator, will choose to aggress instead against others who are *similar* in some way to the frustrator, but against whom it is *less frightening* to aggress. [See Miller (1944 and 1951) for a detailed discussion of how the individual selects the target for his displaced aggression. According to Miller, which of the many substitute targets available to a person is chosen depends on how frustrated the individual is, how frightened he is of aggressing against his frustrator, and on how similar various potential targets are to his frustrator.]

A graphic example of the way aggression can be displaced along the lines of similarity is provided by Mowrer (as reported in Dollard *et al.*, 1939). They report:

> A small boy in an institution displayed unusually strong aggression against adults. This took the form of biting, pinching, and hair-pulling. Under the severe discipline of the institution, this overt aggression was soon inhibited by expectation of punishment. Then the child began running after other children, biting them, pinching them, pulling their hair. These manifestations of aggression were in turn eliminated, in fact so thoroughly that the child ceased biting altogether, even refusing to bite into solid food. Then the child commenced to pinch himself, bang his head, and to pull out his own hair. These actions were so injurious that he created bad sores on his body and two large bald spots on his head . . . *

According to the authors "this case appears to present a picture of frustration imposed by adults, aggression against adults, inhibition of this aggression and displacement of it to other children, inhibition of the aggression against other children and turning of it, still with much the same responses, against the self" (p. 49).

Many experiments have demonstrated that frustrated individuals will displace aggression to minority groups, who are less likely than the frustrator to retaliate against them. One such classic experiment was done by Miller and Bugelski (1948). Their subjects were boys in the Civilian Conservation Corps who were working in an isolated area. The boys' main entertainment each week was attending Bank Night at a movie in town. One

---

*Dollard, J., L. Doob, N. Miller, O. Mowrer, and R. Sears. *Frustration and Aggression.* New Haven: Yale University Press, 1939.

Bank Night, before it was time to leave for the movie, the boys were required to take some very difficult tests. Included in the tests were some items intended to measure their attitudes towards various nationality groups, including Mexicans and Japanese. As the time for the movie approached and then passed, the tests kept coming. Missing the movie was undoubtedly a severe frustration for the boys. Since the boys could not directly attack the experimenters, the researchers expected that the boys would displace their aggression to members of the salient minority groups. The data supported this hypothesis. After it became obvious that the movie had been missed, the boys were again asked some questions about their attitudes toward minority group members. The questionnaire results indicated that after the frustrating experience the boys expressed more unfavorable attitudes toward foreigners than they had expressed previously.

Cowen, Landes, and Schaet (1959) replicated these results. They found that subjects who had been insulted expressed more hostile attitudes towards Negroes than did individuals who had not been frustrated.

There is also correlational evidence that individuals who are frustrated by unknown or invulnerable sources do tend to express more aggression toward individuals who are not responsible for their frustration. Bettelheim and Janowitz (1950) interviewed World War II veterans, and classified them as to their hostility towards Jews and Negroes. Prejudiced attitudes were found to be related to a deterioration in the veterans' social status. Those men who held jobs of a lower social status after the war than they had before the war were more strongly hostile toward minority-group members than were veterans whose occupational opportunities had improved.

In a survey conducted by Campbell (summarized in G. W. Allport, 1954, p. 224), people who were dissatisfied with their jobs were found to be more anti-Semitic than were people who were contented with their employment. That Negroes may be the target of displaced aggression is suggested by the correlations reported earlier between economic conditions and the number of lynchings.

A few experiments indicate that frustrated individuals do not inevitably aggress against minority groups. Stagner and Congdon (1955) angered college students; students were not found to dislike minority-group members more after the frustrating experience than were control subjects.

We have stated in several places the popular assumption that frustrated individuals who cannot aggress against their frustrator directly will displace their aggression to someone who is similar to him in some way. Obviously substitute targets can be similar to the frustrator on any dimensions on which it is possible to categorize individuals. It is surprising to discover that similarities which we might think of as very minor turn out to be important determinants of where a frustrated individual will displace his aggression.

Berkowitz (1968) reports two ingenious studies done in collaboration with Knurek which document this point. In one experiment, men were prevented from winning money by the incompetence of their partner.

Subsequently, the frustrated men were asked to evaluate a second person. Men were found to attribute more unfavorable characteristics to the innocent bystander if he happened to possess the same first name as the frustrator than if he possessed a neutral name. Similarly, in a second experiment, subjects were insulted by another. Subsequently, they were given an opportunity to administer electric shocks to a second person who was innocent of any harm-doing. Frustrated subjects (compared to non-aroused control subjects) gave more shocks to the bystander only when he had the same name as the frustrator.

# CHAPTER EIGHT

# *Courtship and Love*

"Love is such a tissue of paradoxes, and exists in such an endless variety of forms and shades, that you may say almost anything about it that you please, and it is likely to be correct." (Finck, 1891, p. 224.)

Though a voluminous literature exists on the antecedents of interpersonal attraction and repulsion, little experimental research exists to tell us about the antecedents of a strong form of interpersonal attraction—romantic love. For purposes of discussion, we will accept Goode's (1959) definition of love: "A strong emotional attachment, a cathexis, between adolescents or adults of opposite sexes, with at least the components of sex desire and tenderness."

There are several reasons for the surprising dearth of literature in an area of such importance. First, some sociologists and anthropologists have been skeptical that "love" exists with any frequency. For example, Linton (1936) commented:

All societies recognize that there are occasional violent emotional attachments between persons of opposite sex, but our present American culture is practically the only one which has attempted to capitalize on these, and make them the basis for marriage . . . The hero of the modern American movie is always a romantic lover, just as the hero of the old Arab epic is always an epileptic. A cynic may suspect that in any ordinary population the percentage of individuals with a capacity for romantic love of the Hollywood type was about as large as that of persons able to throw genuine epileptic fits (p. 175).

Secondly, those researchers who have believed that love is an important topic to examine have faced unusual difficulties in studying the phenomenon. Until fairly recently, experimental research into romantic love has been almost taboo. For example, in the 1920's two professors at a state university were fired because they approved a questionnaire on attitudes toward sex. The recent pioneering work of Masters and Johnson (1966) has undoubtedly negated the assumption that sexual attraction is not a scientifically respectable topic. Yet, even now that the study of sexual and romantic love has become acceptable, researchers have continued to find it unusually difficult to conduct research in this area. Romantic love occurs less frequently than milder forms of interpersonal attraction. In addition, love usually requires a fairly long period of time to develop. Thus, researchers typically have found it difficult to devise experiments to secure information concerning the antecedents of love (dating, courtship, and marriage). They have usually felt it necessary to limit themselves to survey data, field studies, and other correlational techniques. Usually, making interpretations of cause-and-effect relationships from such data is difficult or impossible.

The bulk of the laboratory research which has been done on romantic attraction has considered possible determinants of one's romantic choices.

## CHOICE OF A ROMANTIC PARTNER

The reasoning, if there is any, behind one's romantic choices is often not apparent to others. One frequently hears the query, "What in the world does he see in her?" Several researchers have speculated that individuals may decide whom to date or whom to like after carefully estimating their own social desirability; that one's decision as to whom he wants for a romantic partner is based on his perception of whom he can get.

It will be recalled that Goffman (1952) argued that "a proposal of marriage in our society tends to be a way in which a man sums up his social attributes and suggests to a woman that hers are not so much better as to preclude a merger or partnership in these matters" (p. 456). This notion suggests that one's romantic feelings, or at least his romantic choices, are affected by both the objective desirability of the other and by one's perceptions of the possibility of attaining the affection of the other.

A number of experimenters have investigated this proposition. The data suggest that while there may be a very slight tendency for individuals to try to date individuals of approximately their own "social worth," this tendency is not very pronounced. Several studies found no evidence that individuals take their own attractiveness into account when deciding whether or not to approach a date. Only one study demonstrated a tendency for individuals to be "realistic" when making their romantic choices.

Walster, Aronson, Abrahams, and Rottmann (1966) conducted a field experiment to test the hypothesis that one's romantic aspirations are influenced by the same realistic considerations that affect one's level of aspiration in other areas.

## Level-of-Aspiration Theory

To understand the authors' predictions, it is necessary to review Level-of-Aspiration Theory (see Lewin, Dembo, Festinger, and Sears, 1944). In their discussion of *"ideal choices,"* Lewin *et al.* state that one's ideal goals are usually based entirely on the desirability of the goal, with no consideration given to the possibility of attaining the goal. One's *"realistic"* level of aspiration, on the other hand, depends both on the objective desirability of the goal *and* on the perceived possibility of attaining that goal. One presumably takes his own skills into account when setting the goal. The authors argue that since the attractiveness of a goal and the probability of attaining that goal are negatively correlated, the goal an individual can expect to attain is usually less attractive than the one he would desire to attain.

Walster *et al.* felt that the choice of a romantic partner parallels in many ways the choice of any goal. The pursuit of a romantic partner is a task which can vary in difficulty. An individual's fantasied romantic choices, like ideal goals, probably are based entirely on the desirability of the object. The choice of a romantic partner, however, would seem to require one to set a more realistic goal. A partner's attractiveness and her availability would seem to be negatively correlated. The more abstractly desirable a potential romantic partner is, the more competition there probably is for her (or him), and the less likely it is that a given individual will be able to attain her friendship. Thus, one's *realistic* social choices should be less "socially desirable" than one's *fantasy* social choices. One's own social attractiveness should affect his romantic level of aspiration.

## The Hypotheses

Reasoning that Level-of-Aspiration theory would apply to romantic choices, the authors proposed the following hypotheses:

1. Individuals who are themselves very socially desirable (physically attractive, personable, possessing great fame or material assets, etc.) will require that a romantic partner possess more social desirability than will a less desirable individual.

2. If couples varying in social desirability meet in a social situation, those couples who are similar in social desirability will most often attempt to date one another.

3. In addition, the authors proposed that an individual will not only *choose* a date of approximately his own social desirability, but also that after actual experience with potential dates of various desirabilities, he will express the most *liking* for a partner of approximately his own desirability.

This last prediction was not directly derived from level-of-aspiration formulations. Aspiration theory deals simply with predicting the choice of a task to perform. Lewin *et al.* predict only that an individual will choose a goal of intermediate attractiveness and difficulty; they do not propose that an individual will come to *like* goals of intermediate difficulty. However, Walster *et al.* reasoned that desirable but unattainable individuals might be derogated, even though other inappropriately difficult tasks might not be, for two reasons: First, if a man chooses an inappropriately difficult task and then fails to attain it, all he suffers is defeat. The task cannot point out to him that he has been presumptuous in choosing a goal so far beyond his level of ability. However, an extremely desirable date can probably be counted on to make it clear to a somewhat undesirable individual that he is foolish to try to win her friendship and that he should not embarrass her by making further overtures. Second, it is likely that an extremely attractive date would not be as considerate of an unattractive date as would a date more similar to himself in attractiveness.

### Designing the Experiment

These hypotheses were tested in a field study involving seven hundred and fifty-two college students who were recruited to attend a freshman dance, for which partners were to be matched by computer. When the freshman arrived to purchase his ticket, his physical attractiveness was surreptitiously rated by a group of college sophomores. (One's "social desirability" is of course made up of many things besides his physical attractiveness. Social desirability includes such attributes as personableness, intelligence, fame, material resources, etc. The authors chose physical attractiveness as the indicator of the subject's social desirability because this particular trait could be quickly assessed under standard conditions by the subject's peers. Data indicate that physical attractiveness ratings are strongly related to one's own perception of his social desirability, so such an index appears to be an appropriate one.)

Freshmen filled out several questionnaires which provided a great deal of other information about them. Ages (nearly all were 18), height, race, and religious preference were obtained. Also assessed were: The students' popularity (a self-report), their expectations in a computer date (how physically attractive, how personally attractive, and how considerate they expected their dates to be), and their self-esteem. From the University's state-wide testing service program at the University of Minnesota, several additional measures were secured. The student's high-school academic percentile rank, his *Minnesota Scholastic Aptitude Test* (MSAT) score, his *Minnesota Multiphasic Personality Inventory* (MMPI) scores, and his *Minnesota Counseling Inventory* (MCI) scores were secured.

Two days after the student completed his questionnaire, he was randomly assigned to a date. The dance was held in a large armory. The couples generally arrived at the dance at 8:00 P.M. and danced or talked until the 10:30 P.M. intermission. During intermission, students' impressions of their dates were assessed. How often couples actually dated was determined six months after the dance.

## Results of the Experiment

It will be recalled that the authors' first prediction was that a subject who was very attractive would expect a "suitable" or "acceptable" date to possess more physical and personal charm and to be more considerate than would a less attractive subject. The data confirm this first hypothesis. There were two ways of testing whether or not attractive subjects did, in fact, expect more of their dates than did less attractive subjects. First, before the subject was assigned to a date, he was asked how physically attractive, how personally attractive, and how considerate he expected his date to be. The more attractive the subject, the more attractive, personable, and considerate he expected his date to be. Second, the subjects rated their liking for their dates during the intermission. Since partners were randomly assigned to one another, very attractive individuals should have had partners who were as attractive, on the average, as the average or unattractive individuals had. In spite of the fact that there were no objective differences in the attractiveness of partners assigned to attractive or unattractive subjects, the attractive students (male and female) consistently judged their dates more harshly than did unattractive students.

Hypothesis 2 proposed that an individual would most often choose to date a partner of approximately his own attractiveness. Hypothesis 3 stated that if individuals were to interact with partners of varying physical attractiveness in a naturalistic setting, an individual would like better, and would more often want to continue to date, a partner similar to himself in attractiveness. Figure 8.1 depicts graphically the theoretical expectation that subjects will most often choose and most often like dates of approximately their own attractiveness. The data did not support Hypotheses 2 and 3. Subjects did not over-rate partners of approximately their own social desirability level.

*Physical attractiveness.* This experiment secured additional results which deserve comment. (It should be noted at this point that all of the findings we will report in connection with this study were equally true for *both* men and women. We have phrased all findings in the masculine gender only to save repetition.)

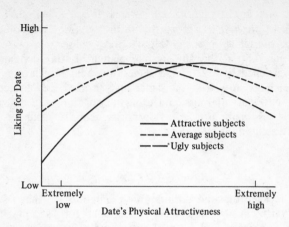

Fig. 8.1. Amount of liking predicted for dates of various attractiveness by ugly, average, and attractive subjects.

1.   Although most of us probably feel we can easily tell how attractive another person is, there was not as much agreement among raters as to who was attractive and who was not, as one might expect. The attractiveness ratings made by the four raters of the same individual had minimal reliability; correlations ranged from .49 to .58.

These correlations do not improve when we compare only the ratings of raters of the same sex. Individuals often feel that two men will agree more about how attractive a woman is than a man and a woman would. The data indicate that this is not so; correlations were about the same regardless of whether raters of the same sex or of opposite sexes were making the rating.

2.   It was also surprising how important physical attractiveness seems to be in determining attraction on the first date. In spite of the fact that the attractiveness ratings had reliabilities of only .49 to .58, the correlation between a date's attractiveness rating and the partner's liking for her ranged from .36 to .44. When we examine the relationship between the individual's own estimation of the date's physical attractiveness and his expression of liking for her, the correlations are still higher (.69 to .78). It is clear that physical attractiveness was by far the most important determinant of how much a date would be liked by her partner.

One might assume that physical attractiveness would have less of an effect on how much a man was liked than on how much a woman was liked. Surprisingly enough, however, it appears that physical attractiveness is just as important an asset for a man as for a woman. The more attractive the date was, regardless of sex, the more his partner liked him and the more often the partner said she wanted to date him again. In addition, the size of these effects was virtually identical for both sexes.

The authors considered various possible alternative explanations for the singular importance of physical attractiveness in determining likability. First, they note that it is known from developmental studies of intelligent individuals (Terman, 1925, 1947, and 1959) that intelligence, physical attractiveness, creativity, and certain personality traits tend to go together. Thus one might argue that it is not really physical attractiveness that was of crucial importance in affecting liking, but one of the correlates of attractiveness. From the evidence, however, it appears that "intelligence" and "personality" are not better predictors of liking than physical attractiveness.

*Intelligence and achievement measures.* Students' high-school percentile ranks and MSAT scores were much more reliable measures than was the measure of physical attractiveness. Yet intelligence was not a variable of the same importance as physical attractiveness in determining liking. In no case did a subject's intelligence significantly affect his date's liking for him.

*Personality measures.* Subjects also completed several personality measures which could be expected to affect the liking they would engender in a social situation. These tests were the Social Relationships (SR) scale of the MCI, the masculinity-femininity scale of the MMPI, the Social introversion (Si) scale of the MMPI, and Berger's *Scale of Self-Acceptance* (1952). None of these personality measures was as good a predictor of liking as was the crude measure of physical attractiveness. Individuals who scored low on these personality tests were slightly better liked by their dates than were high-scoring individuals. However, these correlations were so small as to be almost nonexistent. Personality measures, like intelligence measures, appeared to be very inadequate predictors of liking.

It is, of course, possible that intelligence and personality determinants would have been more important had individuals had more time to get acquainted. It may be that two and a half hours was too short a time for individuals to discover much about their partner's intelligence or personality, while physical attractiveness was obvious from the start. It is not likely, however, that intelligence or personality variables "really" underlie the correlations obtained between attractiveness and romantic liking. It might also be true that physical attractiveness loses some of its importance as individuals get to be older than the 18-year-olds interviewed in this study.

## COUNTERINDICATIONS FOR RECIPROCAL LIKING

The results of this study indicate, then, that the happy accommodation which was proposed between what an individual can realistically hope to attain and what he comes to desire, appears not to exist. The lack of symmetry between the individual's liking for his date and the date's liking for the individual is striking. The correlation between how much a man likes his partner and how much she likes him was virtually zero ($r = .03$). This is especially surprising in view of the fact that one of the strongest determinants of liking we discussed previously was reciprocity—individuals tend to like those who like them.

How can we explain the peculiar fact that whether or not a romantic partner likes one does not seem to affect one's liking for the partner? Perhaps in this situation, individuals were not very affected by their dates' liking for them because the dates were so polite that it was impossible for the individual to know if he was accepted or rejected. Or perhaps individuals were so eager to be liked that they did not want to correctly perceive the available cues. The evidence does not really support these possibilities. Subjects were not oblivious to their partners' feelings about them, even though they could not estimate their liking with great accuracy. (The correlation between the partner's stated liking for the subject and the subject's perception of the partner's liking for him was .23 for male subjects and .36 for female subjects.) Subjects, then, could assess their partner's feelings for them with some accuracy. The other's feeling about them simply did not affect their liking for the other. Why a variable that is usually found to be so important was totally ineffective in a dating situation is puzzling.

From the preceding study, and from four unreported laboratory experiments, we have been led to conclude:

1. That more socially desirable people are harsher in their judgments of others than are socially undesirable people.

2. That there is no tendency for individuals to over-choose partners of approximately their own social desirability. It appears that everyone prefers the most attractive date possible, regardless of his own social desirability, and regardless of the possibility of being rejected by the most attractive date.

The fact that physical attractiveness and social status may have an overriding importance on first acquaintance regardless of one's own level of attractiveness has been noted in survey research. Burgess, Wallin, and Shultz (1953) observe that though dating is satisfactory for the minority of very attractive men and women, it presents severe problems for slightly less attractive individuals. They quote a typical college student.

"One of the greatest troubles is that men here, as everywhere, I guess, are easily overwhelmed by physical beauty. Campus glamor girls have countless beaux flocking around them, whereas many companionable, sympathetic girls who want very much to be companions and, eventually wives and mothers, but who are not dazzling physically, go without dates and male companionship. Many who could blossom out and be very charming never have the opportunity. Eventually, they decide that they are unattractive and become discouraged to the point that often they will not attend no-date functions where they have their best (and perhaps only) opportunity to meet men. I will never understand why so many men (even, or maybe particularly, those who are the least personally attractive themselves) seem to think they may degrade themselves by dating or even dancing with a girl who does not measure up to their beauty standards" (p. 63-64).

Only one study has produced some evidence that one's own social desirability might affect his choice of a romantic partner. Kiesler and Baral (in press) also proposed that realistic behavior should entail choosing a person who is similar in attractiveness to oneself, since by choosing a person similar in over-all favorability one can maximize the attractiveness of his partner while minimizing the risk of rejection. They found support for this hypothesis in an ingenious experiment.

Male subjects were paid to participate in a one-hour study on intelligence testing. In a Raised Self-esteem condition the experimenter attempted to convey to the men the impression that their performance was extremely good. In a Low Self-esteem condition, the experimenter attempted to convey the impression that he was displeased with the man's poor performance.

After a segment of the intelligence test had been completed, the experimenter suggested a coffee break. The experimenter and male subjects went down to a small canteen to buy some coffee. In the canteen, the experimenter appeared to recognize a girl seated at a nearby table and approached her. The girl was actually a confederate. She was introduced to the subject as a coed at a nearby college who was doing summer work for a psychologist at Yale. The physical attractiveness of the girl varied between conditions. In the Attractive condition, the confederate, who actually was highly attractive, wore becoming make-up and fashionable clothing designed to enhance her appearance. In the Unattractive condition, an attempt was made to reduce her initial attractiveness. She wore no make-up, heavy glasses, and had her hair pulled back with a rubber band. Her skirt and blouse, of clashing colors, were arranged sloppily. After the couple was introduced, the experimenter excused himself briefly, and a pre-programmed conversation was begun. The girl began talking to the boy in a friendly, accepting, and interested way.

The extent to which the subject displayed interest in the confederate was the dependent measure. If the subject asked the girl for a date, asked for information which presumably would lead to a date (e.g., asked for her phone number), offered to buy a snack or coffee for her, or ignored her when she said she should "get back to work," he was given points on an index of "romantic behavior."

Kiesler and Baral predicted that subjects' self-esteem would interact with the physical attractiveness of the date in determining romantic behavior. Raised self-esteem subjects were expected to display more romantic behavior towards the girl when she appeared to be highly attractive than when she seemed somewhat unattractive. Lowered self-esteem subjects were expected to display more romantic behavior toward the girl when she seemed unattractive than when she seemed highly attractive. This hypothesis was supported.

These studies lead us to the conclusion that though on some occasions changes in one's self-esteem may affect how attractive a romantic partner one chooses, in many situations changes in self-esteem have been found to have a negligible effect on one's choices. Obviously, further research is necessary to pinpoint which factors make one's own desirability a determinant of one's romantic choices.

*References*

# References

Abelson, R. P., and M. J. Rosenberg. "Symbolic psycho-logic: a model of attitudinal cognition," *Behav. Sci.*, 1958, **3**, 1-13.

Abrams, R. H. "Residential propinquity as a factor in marriage selection," *Amer. Sociol. Rev.*, 1943, **8**, 288-294.

Adler, A. *The Neurotic Constitution.* New York: Dodd, Mead, 1926.

Allport, G. W. *The Nature of Prejudice.* Reading, Mass.: Addison-Wesley, 1954.

Argyle, M. *The Psychology of Interpersonal Behavior.* Baltimore: Penguin, 1967.

Aronson, E., and D. Linder. "Gain and loss of esteem as determinants of interpersonal attractiveness," *J. Exp. Soc. Psych.*, 1965, **1**, 156-171.

Aronson, E. and J. Mills. "The effect of severity of initiation on liking for a group," *J. Abn. Soc. Psych.*, 1959, **67**, 31-36.

Aronson, E. and P. Worchel. "Similarity *vs.* liking as determinants of interpersonal attractiveness," *Psychonomic Sci.*, 1966, **5**, 157-158.

Arsenian, J. M. "Young children in an insecure situation," *J. Abn. Soc. Psych.*, 1943, **38**, 225-249.

Back, K. W. and M. D. Bogdonoff. "Plasma lipid responses to leadership, conformity, and deviation." In P. H. Leiderman and D. Shapiro (Eds.) *Psychobiological Approaches to Social Behavior.* Stanford, Calif.: Stanford Univer. Press, 1964, 36-39.

Backman, C. W. and P. F. Secord. "The effect of perceived liking on interpersonal attraction," *Hum. Rel.*, 1959, **12**, 379-384.

Baldwin, J. *The Fire Next Time.* New York: Dial, 1964, p. 34.

Banta, T. J. and M. Hetherington. "Relations between needs of friends and fiancees," *J. Abn. Soc. Psych.,* 1963, **66**, 401-404.

Bandura, A. and R. H. Walters. *Social Learning and Personality Development.* New York: Holt, Rinehart and Winston, 1963.

Bartlett, R. G., Jr., V. C. Bohr, R. H. Helmendach, G. L. Foster, and M. A. Miller. "Evidence of an emotional factor in hypothermia produced by restraint," *Amer. J. Physiol.,* 1954, **179**, 343-346.

Bartlett, R. G., Jr., R. H. Helmendach, and V. C. Bohr. "Effect of emotional stress, anesthesia, and death on body temperature of mice exposed to cold," *Proc. Soc. Exp. Biol., N. Y.,* 1953, **83**, 4-5.

Bartlett, R. G., Jr., R. H. Helmendach, and W. I. Inman. "Effect of restraint on temperature regulation in the cats," *Proc. Soc. Exp. Biol., N. Y.,* 1954, **85**, 81-83.

Becker, G. "The complementary-need hypothesis: authoritarianism, dominance and other Edwards Personality Preference Schedule scores," *J. Pers.,* 1964, **32**, 45-56.

Beier, E. G., A. M. Rossi, and R. L. Garfield. "Similarity plus dissimilarity of personality: basis for friendship?" *Psych. Rep.,* 1961, 8, 3-8.

Bell, A. G. "Upon the formation of a deaf variety of the human race," *Mem. Nat. Acad. Sci.,* 1883, 2, 179-262.

Berger, E. M., "The relation between expressed acceptance of self and expressed acceptance of others," *J. Abn. Soc. Psych.,* 1952, **47**, 778-782.

Bergler, E. *Divorce Won't Help.* New York: Harper and Brothers, 1948.

Berkowitz, L. "Some aspects of observed aggression," *J. Pers. Soc. Psych.,* 1965, **2**, 359-369.

Berkowitz, L. *Roots of Aggression: A Re-Examination of the Frustration-Aggression Hypothesis.* New York: Atherton Press, 1969.

Berkowitz, L. and L. R. Daniels. "Responsibility and dependency," *J. Abn. Soc. Psych.,* 1963, **66**, 429-436.

Berkowitz, L. and J. A. Green. "The stimulus qualities of the scapegoat," *J. Abn. Soc. Psych.,* 1962, **64**, 293-301.

Berkowitz, L. and D. S. Holmes. "A further investigation of hostility generalization to disliked objects," *J. Pers.,* 1960, **28**, 427-442.

Berkowitz, L. and E. Rawlings. "Effects of film violence on inhibitions against subsequent aggression," *J. Abn. Soc. Psych.,* 1963, **66**, 405-412.

Berscheid, E., D. Boye, and J. M. Darley. "Effects of forced association upon voluntary choice to associate," *J. Pers. Soc. Psych.,* 1968, **8**, 13-19.

Berscheid, E., D. Boye, and E. Walster. "Retaliation as a means of restoring equity," *J. Pers. Soc. Psych.* (in press).

Berscheid, E. and E. Walster. "When does a harm-doer compensate a victim?", *J. Pers. Soc. Psych.,* 1967, **6**, 435-441.

Berscheid, E., E. Walster, and A. Barclay. "The effect of time on the tendency to compensate a victim" (in preparation). Mimeographed copy available from senior author.

Berscheid, E., G. W. Walster, and E. Walster. "Effects of accuracy and positivity of an evaluation on liking for the evaluator " (in preparation). Mimeographed copy available from senior author.

Bettelheim, B. and M. Janowitz. *Dynamics of Prejudice.* New York: Harper, 1950.

Bogardus, E. S. "Measuring social distance," *J. App. Sociol.,* 1925, **9,** 299-308.

Bonney, M. E. "A study of the relationship of intelligence, family size, and sex differences with mutual friendships in primary grades," *Child Devel.,* 1952, **13,** 79-100.

Boroson, W. "What psychiatrists say about Goldwater," *Fact,* 1964, **1,** 24-64.

Bossard, J. H. S. "Residential propinquity as a factor in mate selection," *Amer. J. Sociol.,* 1932, **38,** 219-224.

Boston Psychopathic Hospital. "Experimental psychoses," *Scient. Amer.,* 1955, **192** (6), 34-39.

Bovard, E. W. "The effects of social stimuli on the response to stress," *Psych. Rev.,* 1959, **66,** 267-277.

Bowerman, C. E. and B. R. Day, "A test of the theory of complementary needs as applied to couples during courtship," *Amer. Sociol. Rev.,* 1956, **21,** 602-605.

Bramel, D. "Interpersonal attraction, hostility and perception." In Judson Mills (Ed.) *Experimental social psychology.* New York: Macmillan, 1969.

Bramel, D. "A dissonance-theory approach to defensive projection." *J. Abn. Soc. Psych.,* 1962, **64,** 121-129.

Brehm, J. W. and A. R. Cohen. *Explorations in Cognitive Dissonance.* New York: John Wiley, 1962.

Brock, T. C. and A. H. Buss. "Dissonance, aggression, and evaluation of pain," *J. Abn. Soc. Psych.,* 1962, **65,** 192-202.

Brock, T. C. and A. H. Buss. "Effects of justification for aggression in communication with the victim on post-aggression dissonance," *J. Abn. Soc. Psych.,* 1964, **68,** 403-412.

Broxton, J. A. "A test of interpersonal attraction predictions derived from balance theory," *J. Abn. Soc. Psych.,* 1963, **63,** 394-397.

Burgess, E. W. and P. Wallin. "Homogamy in social characteristics," *Amer. J. Sociol.,* 1943, **49,** 109-124.

Burgess, E. W. and P. Wallin. *Engagement and Marriage.* Philadelphia: Lippincott, 1953.

Burgess, E. W., P. Wallin, and G. D. Shultz. *Courtship, Engagement and Marriage,* Philadelphia: J. B. Lippincott, 1953.

Burnstein, E. and P. Worchel. "Arbitrariness of frustration and its consequences for aggression in a social situation." *J. Pers.,* 1962, **30,** 528-540.

Byrne, D. (a) "The influence of propinquity and opportunities for interaction on classroom relationships," *Hum. Rel.* 1961, **14,** 63-70.

Byrne, D. (b) "Interpersonal attraction and attitude similarity," *J. Abn. Soc. Psych.*, 1961, **62**, 713-715.

Byrne, D. and B. Blaylock, "Similarity and assumed similarity of attitudes between husbands and wives," *J. Abn. Soc. Psych.*, 1963, **67**, 636-640.

Byrne, D. and J. A. Buehler, "A note on the influence of propinquity upon acquaintanceships," *J. Abn. Soc. Psych.*, 1955, **51**, 147-148.

Byrne, D. and G. L. Clore, Jr. "Predicting interpersonal attraction toward strangers presented in three different stimulus modes," *Psych. Sci.*, 1966, **4**, 239-240.

Byrne, D. and W. Griffitt, "A developmental investigation of the law of attraction," *J. Pers. Soc. Psych.*, 1966, **4**, 699-703.

Byrne, D. and W. Griffitt, "Similarity versus liking: A clarification" (in press).

Byrne, D. and D. Nelson, "Attraction as a linear function of proportion of positive reinforcements," *J. Pers. Soc. Psych.*, 1965, **1**, 659-663.

Byrne, D. and T. J. Wong, "Racial prejudice, interpersonal attraction and assumed dissimilarity of attitudes," *J. Abn. Soc. Psych.*, 1962, **65**, 246-252.

Carlsmith, J. M. and A. Gross. "The effect of guilt on compliance with a simple request," *J. Pers. Soc. Psych.* (in press).

Carnegie, D. *How to Win Friends and Influence People.* New York: Simon and Schuster, 1937.

Cartwright, D. and F. Harary. "Structural balance: a generalization of Heider's theory," *Psych. Rev.*, 1956, **63**, 277-293.

Cattell, R. B., E. F. Maxwell, B. H. Like, and M. P. Unger. "The objective measurement of attitudes," *Brit. J. Psych.* 1950, **50**, 235-252.

Cattell, R. B. and J. R. Nesselroade, "Likeness and completeness theories examined by 16 personality factor measures on stably and unstably married couples," *J. Pers. Soc. Psych.*, 1967, **7**, 351-361.

Conger, J. J., W. L. Sawrey, and E. S. Turrell, "An experimental investigation of the role of social experience in the production of gastric ulcers in hooded rats," *Amer. Psych.*, 1957, **12**, 410 (abstract).

Cowen, D., J. Landes, and D. E. Schaet. "The effects of mild frustration on the expression of prejudiced attitudes," *J. Abn. Soc. Psych.*, 1959, **58**, 33-38.

Darley, J. M. and E. Aronson, "Self-evaluation *vs.* direct anxiety reduction as determinants of the fear-affiliation relationship," *J. Exp. Soc. Psych. Suppl.*, 1966, **1**, 66-79.

Darley, J. M. and E. Berscheid, "Increased liking as a result of the anticipation of personal contact," *Hum. Rel.*, 1967, **20**, 29-40.

Davidson, J. "Cognitive familiarity and dissonance reduction," in Leon Festinger (Ed.), *Conflict, Decision, and Dissonance.* Stanford, California: Stanford Press, 1964, 45-60.

Davis, K. E., and E. E. Jones, "Changes in interpersonal perception as a means of reducing cognitive dissonance," *J. Abn. Soc. Psych.*, 1960, **61**, 402-410.

Davitz, J. R. and D. J. Mason, "Socially facilitated reduction of a fear response in rats," *J. Comp. Phys. Psych.*, 1955, **48**, 149-151.

Deutsch, M. and M. E. Collins, "The effect of public policy in housing projects upon interracial attitudes," in Eleanor Maccoby, T. M. Newcomb, and E. L. Hartley (Eds.), *Readings in Social Psychology* (3rd ed.). New York: Holt, 1958, 612-623.

Deutsch, M., and L. Solomon, "Reactions to evaluations by others as influenced by self-evaluation," *Sociometry*, 1959, **22**, 93-112.

Dickoff, H. "Reactions to evaluations by another person as a function of self-evaluation and the interaction context," unpublished doctoral dissertation, Duke University, 1961. Also reported in Jones, E. E., *Ingratiation.* New York: Appleton-Century Crofts, 1964.

Dittes, J. E. "Attractiveness of group as function of self-esteem and acceptance by group," *J. Abn. Soc. Psych.*, 1959, **59**, 77-82.

Dollard, J., L. Doob, N. Miller, O. Mowrer, and R. Sears. *Frustration and Aggression.* New Haven: Yale University Press, 1939.

Dorwart, W., R. Ezerman, M. Lewis, D. Rosenhan. The effect of brief social deprivation on social and nonsocial reinforcement. *J. Pers. Soc. Psych.*, 1965, **2**, 111-115.

Dulany, D. E., Jr. "Hypotheses and habits in verbal 'operant conditioning' " *J. Abn. Soc. Psych.*, 1961, **63**, 251-263.

Dymond, Rosalind. "Interpersonal perception and marital happiness," *Canad. J. Psych.*, 1954, **8**, 164-171.

Edwards, A. L. "Political frames of reference as a factor influencing recognition," *J. Abn. Soc. Psych.*, 1941, **36**, 34-50.

Fay, E. A. *Marriages of the Deaf in America,* Washington (Volta Bureau), 1898.

Festinger, L. "Architecture and group membership," *J. Soc. Iss.*, 1951, **1**, 152-163.

Festinger, L. "Group attraction and membership," in D. Cartwright and A. Zander (Eds.), *Group Dynamics: Research and Theory.* Evanston, Ill.: Row, Peterson, 1953.

Festinger, L. "A theory of social comparison processes," *Hum. Rel.*, 1954, **7**, 117-140.

Festinger, L. *A Theory of Cognitive Dissonance.* Evanston, Ill.: Row, Peterson, 1957.

Festinger, L., A. Pepitone, and T. M. Newcomb. "Some consequences of deindividuation in a group," *J. Abn. Soc. Psych.*, 1952, **47**, 382-389.

Festinger, L., S. Schachter, and K. Back. *Social Pressures in Informal Groups: A Study of Human Factors in Housing.* New York: Harper, 1950.

Finck, H. T. *Romantic Love and Personal Beauty: Their Development, Causal Relations, Historic and National Peculiarities.* London: Macmillan, 1891.

Freedman, J. L., S. A. Wallington, and E. Bless. "Compliance without pressure: the effect of guilt," *J. Pers. Soc. Psych.*, 1967, **7**, 117-124.

Fromm, E., "Selfishness and self-love," *Psychiatry,* 1939, **2**, 507-523.

Garrison, R. J., V. E. Anderson, and S. C. Reed. "Assortative marriage," *Eug. Quart.,* 1968 (in press).

Gerard, E. O. "Medieval Psychology: Dogmatic Aristotelianism or Observational Empiricism?," *J. Hist. Behav. Sci.,* 1966, **2**, 315-329.

Gerard, H. B. and J. M. Rabbie. "Fear and social comparison," *J. Abn. Soc. Psych.,* 1961, **62**, 586-592.

Gewirtz, J. L. and D. M. Baer. (a) "The effect of brief social deprivation on behaviors for a social reinforcer," *J. Abn. Soc. Psych.,* 1958, **56**, 49-56.

Gewirtz, J. L. and D. M. Baer. (b) "Deprivation and satiation of social reinforcers as drive conditions," *J. Abn. Soc. Psych.,* 1958, **57**, 165-172.

Glass, D. C. "Changes in liking as a means of reducing cognitive discrepancies between self-esteem and aggression," *J. Pers.,* 1964, **32**, 531-549.

Goffman, E. "On cooling the mark out: Some aspects of adaptation to failure," *Psychiatry,* 1952, **15**, 451-463.

Goldberg, G. N., C. A. Kiesler, and B. E. Collins. "Interpersonal attraction and situational definition as determinants of the spacing of interacting individuals," *Sociometry* (in press).

Goldschmid, M. L. "Prediction of college majors by personality tests," *J. Couns. Psych.,* 1967, **14**, 302-308.

Goldstein, J. W. and H. Rosenfeld. "Insecurity and preference for persons similar to oneself," *J. Pers.* (in press).

Goode, William J. "The theoretical importance of love," *Amer. Sociol. Rev.,* 1959, **24**, 38-47.

Goranson, R. E. and L. Berkowitz, "Reciprocity and responsibility reactions to prior help," *J. Pers. Soc. Psych.,* 1966, **3**, 227-232.

Greenspoon, J. "The reinforcing effect of two spoken sounds on the frequency of two responses," *Amer. J. Psych.,* 1955, **68**, 409-416.

Gullahorn, J. "Distance and friendship as factors in the gross interaction matrix," *Sociometry,* 1952, **15**, 123-134.

Guttman, L. "A basis for scaling qualitative data," *Amer. Sociol. Rev.,* 1944, **9**, 139-150.

Hamblin, R. "Group integration during a crisis," *Hum. Rel.,* 1958, **11**, 67-76.

Hamblin, R. I., D. A. Bridger, R. C. Day, and W. L. Yancey. "The interference-aggression law?", *Sociometry,* 1963, **26**, 190-216.

Hammond, K. R. "Measuring attitudes by error-choice: an indirect method," *J. Abn. Soc. Psych.,* 1948, **43**, 38-48.

Harris, J. A. "Assortative mating in man," *The Popular Science Monthly,* 1912, **80**, 476-492.

Harvey, O. J. "Personality factors in resolution of conceptual incongruities," *Sociometry,* 1962, **25**, 336-352.

Harvey, O. J., H. H. Kelley, and M. M. Shapiro. "Reactions to unfavorable evaluations of the self made by other persons," *J. Pers.,* 1957, **25**, 393-411.

Heider, F. *The Psychology of Interpersonal Relations.* Wiley, 1958.

Hess, E. W. "Attitude and pupil size," *Sci. Amer.*, 1965, **212**, p. 46.

Hess, E. W. and J. M. Polt. "Pupil size as related to interest value of visual stimuli," *Science,* 1960, **132**, 349-350.

Hoffeditz, E. L. "Family resemblances in personality traits," *J. Soc. Psych.*, 1934, **5**, 214-227.

Hoffman, L. R. "Similarity of personality: a basis for interpersonal attraction?", *Sociometry,* 1958, **21**, 300-308.

Hokanson, J. E. "The effects of frustration and anxiety on overt aggression," *J. Abn. Soc. Psych.*, 1961, **62**, 346-351.

Homans, G. C. *Social Behavior: Its Elementary Forms.* New York: Harcourt, Brace and World, 1961.

Hoover, J. E. "Crime in the United States," *Uniform Crime Reports,* August, 1966, U.S. Dept. of Justice, Washington, D. C.

Horney, K. *New Ways in Psychoanalysis.* New York: Norton, 1939.

Horwitz, M. "The veridicality of liking and disliking," in R. Tagiuri and L. Petrullo (Eds.), *Person Perception and Interpersonal Behavior.* Stanford: Stanford University Press, 1958.

Hovland, C. and R. Sears. "Minor studies in aggression: VI. Correlation of lynchings with economic indices," *J. Psych.*, 1940, **9**, 301-310.

Hunt, A. M. "A study of the relative value of certain ideals," *J. Abn. Soc. Psych.*, 1935, **30**, 222-228.

Izard, C. E. (a) "Personality similarity, positive affect, and interpersonal attraction," *J. Abn. Soc. Psych.*, 1960, **61**, 484-485.

Izard, C. E. (b) "Personality similarity and friendship," *J. Abn. Soc. Psych.*, 1960, **61**, 47-51.

Izard, C. E. "Personality similarity and friendship: a follow up study," *J. Abn. Soc. Psych.*, 1963, **66**, 598-600.

Jacobs, L., E. Walster, and E. Berscheid, "The relation between self-esteem, the assumption of being liked, and romantic attraction" (in preparation). Mimeographed copy available from second author.

James, A. and A. J. Lott, "Reward frequency and the formation of positive attitudes toward group members," *J. Soc. Psych.*, 1964, **62**, 111-115.

Jecker, J. and D. Landy. "Liking a person as a function of doing him a favor," *Hum. Rel.* (in press).

Jones, E. E. *Ingratiation: A Social Psychological Analysis.* Appleton-Century Crofts, New York, 1964.

Jones, E. E., K. J. Gergen, and K. E. Davis. "Some determinants of reactions to being approved or disapproved as a person," *Psych. Mon.*, 1962, **76**, Whole No. 521.

Jones, E. E., R. G. Jones, and K. J. Gergen. "Some conditions affecting the evaluation of a conformist," *J. Pers.*, 1963, **31**, 270-288.

Jones, H. E. "Homogamy in intellectual abilities," *Amer. J. Sociol.*, 1929, **35**, 369-382.

Jones, R. G., and E. E. Jones. "Optimum conformity as an ingratiation tactic," *J. Pers.*, 1964, **32**, 436-458.

Katz, A. M. and R. Hill. "Residential propinquity and marital selection: A review of theory, method, and fact," *Marr. Fam. Liv.*, 1958, **20**, 327-335.

Katz, D. and E. Stotland. "A preliminary statement to a theory of attitude structure and change," in S. Koch (Ed.), *Psychology: A Study of a Science*, Vol. 3, New York: McGraw-Hill, 1959, 423-475.

Katz, I., S. Glucksberg, and R. Krauss. "Need-satisfaction and Edwards PPS scores in married couples," *J. Cons. Psych.*, 1960, **24**, 203-208.

Kennedy, R. "Premarital residential propinquity," *Amer. J. Sociol.*, 1943, **48**, 580-584.

Kerckhoff, A. C. and K. E. Davis. "Value consensus and need complementarity in mate selection," *Amer. Sociol. Rev.*, 1962, **27**, 295-303.

Kiesler, C. A. and G. N. Goldberg. "Multidimensional approach to the experimental study of interpersonal attraction: Effect of a blunder on the attractiveness of a competent other," *Psych. Rep.*, 1968, **22**, 693-705.

Kiesler, C. A. and S. B. Kiesler. *Conformity*. Reading, Mass.: Addison-Wesley, 1969.

Kiesler, S. B. and R. L. Baral. "The search for a romantic partner: The effects of self-esteem and physical attractiveness on romantic behavior" (in press).

Kipnis, D. M. "Interaction between members of bomber crews as a determinant of sociometric choice," *Hum. Rel.*, 1957, **10**, 263-270.

Ktsanes, T. "Mate selection on the basis of personality type: A study utilizing an empirical typology of personality," *Amer. Sociol. Rev.*, 1955, **20**, 547-551.

Latane, B. and D. C. Glass. "Social and nonsocial attraction in rats," *J. Pers. Soc. Psych.*, 1968, **9**, 142-146.

Lerner, M. J. "Evaluation of performance as a function of performer's reward and attractiveness," *J. Pers. Soc. Psych.*, 1965, **1**, 355-360.

Lerner, M. J., and G. Matthews. "Reactions to the suffering of others under conditions of indirect responsibility," *J. Pers. Soc. Psych.*, 1967, **5**, 319-325.

Lerner, M. J. and C. H. Simmons. "Observer's reaction to the 'innocent victim': Compassion or rejection?", *J. Pers. Soc. Psych.*, 1966, **4**, 203-210.

Levine, J. M. and G. Murphy. "The learning and forgetting of controversial material," *J. Abn. and Soc. Psych.*, 1943, **38**, 507-517.

Levinger, G. "Note on need complementarity in marriage," *Psych. Bull.*, 1964, **61**, 153-157.

Levinger, G. and J. Breedlove. "Interpersonal attraction and agreement: A study of marriage partners," *J. Pers. Soc. Psych.*, 1966, **3**, 367-372.

Lewin, K., T. Dembo, L. Festinger, and P. Sears. "Level of aspiration," in J. McV. Hunt (Ed.), *Personality and the Behavior Disorders*. New York: Ronald Press, Vol. 1, 1944, 333-378.

Liddell, H. "Some specific factors that modify tolerance for environmental stress," in H. G. Wolff, S. G. Wolf, Jr. and C. C. Hare (Eds.), *Life Stress and Bodily Disease.* Baltimore: Williams and Wilkins, 1950, 155-171.

Likert, R. "A technique for the measurement of attitudes," *Arch. Psych.,* 1932, **140**, 44-53.

Lindzey, G. and E. F. Borgatta. "Sociometric measurement," in G. Lindzey (Ed.), *Handbook of Social Psychology:* Vol. 1, *Theory and Method.* Cambridge, Mass.: Addison-Wesley, 1954, 405-448.

Linton, R. *The Study of Man.* New York: Appleton-Century, 1936.

Loeblowitz-Lennard, H. and F. Riessman, Jr. "A proposed projective attitude test," *Psychiatry,* 1946, **9**, 67-68.

Lott, A. J. and B. E. Lott. "Group cohesiveness, communication level, and conformity," *J. Abn. Soc. Psych.,* 1961, **62**, 408-412.

Lundy, R. M., W. Katkovsky, R. L. Cromwell, and D. J. Shoemaker. "Self acceptability and descriptions of sociometric choices," *J. Abn. Soc. Psych.,* 1955, **51**, 260-262.

Maisonneuve, J., G. Palmade, and C. Fourment. "Selective choices and propinquity," *Sociometry,* 1952, **15**, 135-140.

Mallick, S. K. and B. R. McCandless. "A study of catharsis of aggression," *J. Pers. Soc. Psych.,* 1966, **4**, 591-596.

Mandlebaum, D. G. *Soldier Groups and Negro Soldiers.* Berkeley: University of California, 1952, 45-48.

Mann, J. H. "The effect of interracial contact on sociometric choices and perceptions," *J. Soc. Psych.,* 1959, **50**, 143-152.

Marshall, R. "Precipitation and presidents," *The Nation,* 1927, **124**, 315-316.

Maslow, A. H. "Self-esteem (dominance feeling) and sexuality in women," *J. Soc. Psych.,* 1942, **16**, 259-294.

Maslow, A. H. "Self-actualizing people; a study in psychological health," *Personality,* 1950, **1**, 11-34.

Maslow, A. H. "Love in healthy people," in A. Montagu (Ed.), *The Meaning of Love.* New York: The Julian Press, 1953.

Mason, W. A. "Socially mediated reduction in emotional responses of young rhesus monkeys," *J. Abn. Soc. Psych.,* 1960, **60**, 100-104.

Masters, W. H. and V. E. Johnson. *Human Sexual Response.* St. Louis: Boston, Little, and Brown, 1966.

Miller, N. E. "The frustration-aggression hypothesis," *Psych. Rev.,* 1941, **48**, 337-342.

Miller, N. E. "Experimental studies of conflict," in J. McV. Hunt (Ed.), *Personality, and the Behavioral Disorders,* New York: Ronald, 1944, 431-465.

Miller, N. E. "Comments on theoretical models illustrated by the development of a theory of conflict," *J. Pers.,* 1951, **20**, 82-100.

Miller, N. E., and R. Bugelski. "Minor studies in aggression: the influence of frustration imposed by the in-group on attitudes expressed toward out-groups," *J. Psych.*, 1948, **25**, 437-442.

Miller, N., D. T. Campbell, H. Twedt, and E. J. O'Connell. "Similarity, contrast, and complementarity in friendship choice," *J. Pers. Soc. Psych.*, 1966, **3**, 3-12.

Moreno, J. L. *Who Shall Survive?* Washington: Nervous and Mental Disease Publishing Co., 1943.

Murstein, B. I. "A complementary need hypothesis in newlyweds and middle-aged married couples," *J. Abn. and Soc. Psych.*, 1961, **63**, 194-197.

Murstein, B. I. "The relationship of mental health to marital choice and courtship progress," *J. Marr. Fam.*, 1967, **29**, 447-451.

Newcomb, T. M. "The influence of attitude climate upon some determinants of information," *J. Abn. Soc. Psych.*, 1946, **41**, 291-302.

Newcomb, T. M. "The prediction of interpersonal attraction," *Amer. Psych.*, 1956, **11**, 575-586.

Newcomb, T. M. *The Acquaintance Process*. New York: Holt, Rinehart and Winston, 1961.

Newcomb, T. and G. Svehla. "Intra-family relationship in attitude," *Sociometry*, 1937, **1**, 180-205.

Omwake, Katherine. "The relationship between acceptance of self and acceptance of others shown by three personality inventories," *J. Cons. Psych.*, 1954, **18**, 443-446.

Ossorio, P. G. and K. E. Davis. "The self, intentionality, and reactions to evaluations of the self," in C. Gordon and K. J. Gergen (Eds.), *Self in Society*. New York: Wiley, 1966.

Palmore, E. B. "The introduction of Negroes into white departments," *Hum. Org.*, 1955, **14**, 27-28.

Parrish, J. A. "The direct and indirect assessment of attitudes as influenced by propagandized radio transcription," Masters' thesis, Ohio State University, 1948.

Pearson, K. and A. Lee. "On the laws of inheritance in man: I. Inheritance of physical characters," *Biometrika*, 1903, **2**, 372-377.

Proust, M. *Swann's Way*. New York: Modern Library, 1928.

Reader, N. and H. B. English. "Personality factors in adolescent female friendships," *J. Cons. Psych.*, 1947, **11**, 212-220.

Reed, E. W. and S. C. Reed. *Mental Retardation: A Family Study*. Philadelphia: W. B. Saunders Co., 1965.

Reik, T. *A Psychologist Looks at Love*. New York: Farrar and Rinehart, 1944.

Richardson, H. M. "Studies of mental resemblance between husbands and wives and between friends," *Psych. Bull.*, 1939, **36**, 104-120.

Rogers, C. R. *Client-centered Therapy*. Boston: Houghton Mifflin, 1951.

Roos, D. E. "Complementary needs in mate-selection: a study based on R-type factor analysis," unpublished Ph. D. dissertation, Northwestern University, 1956.

Rosenberg, M. J. "An analysis of affective-cognitive consistency," in M. J. Rosenberg and C. I. Hovland (Eds.), *Attitude Organization and Change.* New Haven, Conn.: Yale University Press, 1960, 15-64.

Rosow, I. "Issues in the concept of need-complementarity," *Sociometry,* 1957, **20,** 216-233.

Sarnoff, I. and P. G. Zimbardo. "Anxiety, fear, and social affiliation," *J. Abn. Soc. Psych.,* 1961, **62,** 356-363.

Schachter, S. *The Psychology of Affiliation.* Stanford, California: Stanford University Press, 1959.

Schachter, S. and F. Heinzelmann. "Cognition, anxiety, and time perception," cited in Schachter's *The Psychology of Affiliation,* above; pages 47-51.

Schellenberg, J. A., and L. S. Bee. "A re-examination of the theory of complementary needs in mate selection," *Marr. Fam. Liv.,* 1960, **22,** 227-232.

Schooley, M. "Personality resemblances among married couples," *J. Abn. Soc. Psych.,* 1936, **31,** 340-347.

Selye, H. *Stress.* Montreal: Acta, 1950, 267-277.

Shallenberger, P. and E. Zigler. "Rigidity, negative reaction tendencies and cosatiation effects in normal and feeble-minded children," *J. Abn. Soc. Psych.,* 1961, **63,** 20-26.

Sherif, M. and L. W. Sherif. *An Outline of Social Psychology* (rev. ed.). New York: Harper and Row, 1956.

Sherif, M., O. J. Harvey, B. J. White, W. R. Hood, and C. W. Sherif. *Experimental Study of Positive and Negative Intergroup Attitudes between Experimentally Produced Groups. Robbers' Cave Study.* Norman: Univ. of Oklahoma, 1954 (multilithed).

Sigall, H. and E. Aronson. "Opinion change and the gain-loss model of interpersonal attraction," *J. Exp. Soc. Psych.,* 1967, **3,** 178-188.

Stagner, R. and C. S. Congdon. "Another failure to demonstrate displacement of aggression," *J. Abn. Soc. Psych.,* 1955, **51,** 695-696.

Stevenson, H. W., R. Keen, and R. M. Knights. "Parents and strangers as reinforcing agents for children's performance," *J. Abn. Soc. Psych.,* 1963, **65,** 429-431.

Stevenson, H. W. and R. M. Knights. "Social reinforcement with normal and retarded children as a function of pretraining, sex of E, and sex of S," *Amer. J. Ment. Def.,* 1962, **66,** 866-871.

Stevenson, H. W. and R. D. Odom. "The effectiveness of social reinforcement following two conditions of social deprivation," *J. Abn. Soc. Psych.,* 1962, **65,** 429-431.

Stock, D. "An investigation into the intercorrelations between the self-concept and feelings directed toward other persons and groups," *J. Cons. Psych.*, 1949, **13**, 176-180.

Taft, R. "Selective recall and memory distortion of favorable and unfavorable material," *J. Abn. Soc. Psych.*, 1954, **49**, 23-28.

Tagiuri, R. "Social preference and its perception," in R. Tagiuri and L. Petrullo (Eds.), *Person Perception and Interpersonal Behavior.* Stanford: Stanford University Press, 1958, 316-336.

Terman, L. M. *Genetic Studies of Genius,* Vol. 1, Stanford: Stanford University Press, 1925.

Terman, L. M. *Genetic Studies of Genius,* Vol. 4, Stanford: Stanford University Press, 1947.

Terman, L. M. *Genetic Studies of Genius,* Vol. 5, Stanford: Stanford University Press, 1959.

Tharp, R. G. "Psychological patterning in marriage," *Psych. Bull.*, 1963, **60**, 97-117.

Thibaut, J. W. and H. H. Kelley. *The Social Psychology of Groups.* New York: Wiley and Sons, 1959, 89-99.

Thomas, D. S. *Social Aspects of a Business Cycle.* London: Rutledge, 1925.

Thompson, W. R. and R. Nishimura. "Some determinants of friendship," *J. Pers.*, 1952, **20**, 305-314.

Thurstone, L. L. "Attitudes can be measured," *Amer. J. Sociol.*, 1928, **33**, 529-554.

Ulrich, R. "Pain as the cause of aggression," *Amer. Zool.*, 1966, **6**, 643-662.

Walster, E. "The effect of self-esteem on romantic liking," *J. Exp. Soc. Psych.*, 1965, **1**, 184-197.

Walster, E. "The assignment of responsibility for an accident," *J. Pers. Soc. Psych.*, 1966, **3**, 73-79.

Walster, E., V. Aronson, D. Abrahams, and L. Rottmann. "Importance of physical attractiveness in dating behavior," *J. Pers. Soc. Psych.*, 1966, **5**, 508-516.

Walster, E., E. Berscheid, and A. N. Barclay. "A determinative of preference for modes of dissonance reduction," *J. Pers. Soc. Psych.*, 1967, **7**, 211-215.

Walster, E. and P. Prestholdt. "The effect of misjudging another: Overcompensation or dissonance reduction?", *J. Exp. Soc. Psych.*, 1966, **2**, 85-97.

Walster, E. and G. W. Walster. "Effect of expecting to be liked on choice of associates," *J. Abn. Soc. Psych.*, 1963, **67**, 402-404.

Walster, E., G. W. Walster, D. Abrahams, and Z. Brown. "The effect on liking of underrating or overrating another," *J. Exp. Soc. Psych.*, 1966, **2**, 70-84.

Watson, W. S. and G. W. Hartman. "The rigidity of a basic attitudinal frame," *J. Abn. Soc. Psych.*, 1939, **34**, 314-335.

Webb, E. J., D. T. Campbell, R. D. Schwartz, and L. Sechrest. *Unobtrusive Measures: Nonreactive Research in the Social Sciences.* Chicago: Rand McNally and Co., 1966.

Weiss, W. "A 'sleeper' effect in opinion change," *J. Abn. Soc. Psych.,* 1953, **48,** 173-180.

Willerman, B. and L. Swanson. "An ecological determinant of differential amounts of sociometric choices within college sororities," *Sociometry,* 1952, **15,** 326-329.

Winch, R. F. *The Modern Family.* New York: Holt, 1952.

Winch, R. F., T. Ktsanes, and V. Ktsanes. "The theory of complementary needs in mate selection: an analytic and descriptive study," *Amer. Sociol. Rev.,* 1954, **19,** 241-249.

Zajonc, R. B. "The concepts of balance, congruity, and dissonance," *Pub. Opin. Quart.,* 1960, **24,** 280-286.

Zander, A. and A. Havelin. "Social comparison and interpersonal attraction," *Hum. Rel.,* 1960, **13,** 21-32.

Zimbardo, P. G. and R. Formica. "Emotional comparison and self-esteem as determinants of affiliation," *J. Pers.,* 1963, **31,** 141-162.